A LITTLE
STYLE
BOOK

CARIBBEAN STYLE

SUZANNE SLESIN AND STAFFORD CLIFF,
JACK BERTHELOT, MARTINE GAUMÉ,
DANIEL ROZENSZTROCH

PHOTOGRAPHS BY
GILLES DE CHABANEIX

CLARKSON POTTER/PUBLISHERS   NEW YORK

Thank you again to all the people who allowed us to photograph their homes on the islands represented in Caribbean Style; *to our agent, Barbara Hogenson of the Lucy Kroll Agency; Beth Gardiner, our editorial assistant; Ian Hammond, our art associate; Howard Klein, art director of Clarkson Potter, and Renato Stanisic, designer; Joan Denman and Andrea C. Peabbles; and our editor, Roy Finamore, who made sure that this new* Caribbean Style, *although smaller in size, was just as consistently strong as the original.*

Manufactured in China

Design by Renato Stanisic

Library of Congress Catalog Number 94-20070

ISBN 0-517-88216-7

10 9 8 7 6 5 4 3 2 1

Revised Edition

CONTENTS

INTRODUCTION

The Caribbean. The place immediately brings to mind specific colors, arranged in a specific way. Blue above, blue below. White for the beach, green for the coconut palms. Dominating all, the gold of the sun. This little book will add to that palette the colors and shades of the lives of a people seen through their homes.

All West Indians, whether they live on the Bahamas to the north or the Greater or Lesser Antilles to the south, are the descendants of transplanted peoples. Spaniards lured by dreams of gold were the primary conquerors of the Caribbean. Then, slowly, the English and French began to colonize the Lesser Antilles, which the Spaniards had ignored. From the 1600s until the mid-19th century, millions of enslaved Africans were convoyed to the islands. Others emigrated from far-off Asia. All were forced to reeducate themselves in order to survive. The conditions they met were often unbearable, but out of their struggles and efforts a Creole culture and a Creole way of life were born.

The early settlers built only temporary shelters. They clung to the idea of one day returning to their homelands. But with the development of the sugar trade, permanent homes were constructed. The grandest houses in the Antilles were built with wealth derived from sugarcane. Many of them have completely disappeared or fallen into ruin. Those that remain are fragile relics of a bygone world and are today in danger of disappearing with the death of the sugar trade.

The first characteristics of a truly Caribbean style appeared during the 18th century. But it was only in the following century that a fully coherent, specifically Caribbean architecture developed. Caribbean style represents a vernacular architecture without official agreement or approval. It is not involved with learned concepts and does not frequent the seats of academe. It is a truly living style and is the fruit of experience. The diverse components group themselves as for a painting. Above the thickets, the royal palms, which once provided wood for construction, are evidence of long-gone settlements. The tamarind, which offers restful shade and whose fruit is rich in vitamin C, is planted today, as long ago, between the house and the kitchen—which were traditionally located in different buildings, as a protection against fire.

This book is certain to be a surprise for West Indians themselves. They live on their own islands, in a kind of exile from all the other islands. Each island is considered by its inhabitants a world unto itself, the far-off colony of a Western power. They are not acquainted with one another, and in any case, they believe that what is best in themselves comes from Europe or elsewhere. In these pages, West Indians will discover an undeniable, deep-rooted common Creole heritage.

It is their Creole identity that unites these cultures born in the conquest of the New World and anchored in islands of the Americas. Their wealth is drawn from their diversity.

PRECEDING PAGES: *Rose Hall Great House was built about 5 miles east of Montego Bay in Jamaica between 1770 and 1780.*

People of the Caribbean

To become familiar with the people of the Caribbean, it is not sufficient merely to enter the homes of the upper classes. Christmas wreaths that last all year, children's balloons, and highly colored prints are just some of the things that enliven the interiors of simple residences—just as the exteriors of the houses are brightened by sharp, lively colors. The houses of the townspeople and peasants, as well the buildings created in the service of colonial powers, have stories to tell.

Jan Morris, the well-known English author, has written that the Caribbean islands "have been variously ruled by the French, the Spaniards, the English, the Dutch, the Danes and the Americans, and some indeed have been passed so repeatedly from sovereignty to sovereignty that they are a positive mish-mash of influences and memories; while the great black majority of the populace, descended from African slaves, have acquired over the generations myriad ethnic strains and symptoms, from the high cheekbones of the original Carib Indians to the commanding postures of European aristocrats."

The architectural style of the Caribbean was developed by borrowing from the different cultures that were in contact throughout the islands. Elements of Creole architecture that can be traced to the colonists include jalousie shutters and the symmetrical composition of façades organized around a central entrance. The French brought dormer windows, and only on the islands colonized by the English is the taste for porches prevalent. The Spanish built houses of very simple forms.

Finally, some characteristics were provided by the black populations who were brought over into slavery. As in Africa, the blacks of the Antilles preferred darkness in the interiors of their cabins and closed them hermetically. This African custom was reinforced by the circumstances of slavery. The slave had nothing that really belonged to him. The interior of his house was the single element of his life over which he had some control.

PRECEDING PAGES: *Students on Marie-Galante, an island that is part of Guadeloupe, study with a semiretired schoolteacher.*

Above: *On Haiti, people live in houses where the roofs and sides are made of royal palms, a building material that was used by the Amerindians.* **Left:** *An owner of a house in Grand Fonds, on Guadeloupe, visits with a family friend on the verandah.*

CLOCKWISE FROM TOP LEFT: *A Haitian farmer surveys the expansive view from the small garden near his house. On Haiti, a man is half hidden in a grove of mango trees. Oxen pull a cart on Marie-Galante—a typical Antillean scene. A child stands on the wide stone steps at the rear of the Alexandra Hotel, on Haiti. Another child plays near the rear gallery of a house on Antigua.*

*On the balcony of an old house
in the center of Point-à-Pitre,
on Guadeloupe, the children
of the family pose near pots of
blooming bougainvillea.*

Narrow roads on which people travel on foot or by motorbike link villages throughout the Caribbean.

Wooden boats, often outfitted with outboard motors and topped with an elaborate system of fishnets, are a common sight.

ABOVE: *Members of the hotel staff of the Alexandra Hotel on Haiti stand by the entrance to the original kitchen, which is housed in a separate building from the main house.* **LEFT:** *A child peeks out of the window of a pastel house on Nevis.*

The house of a retired school-teacher on Marie-Galante was built by a carpenter for his sister. A craftsman's master-piece, it is considered a fine example of local folk art.

ABOVE: *A bus, with its rooftop load, makes its way through a crowded Haitian marketplace.* **RIGHT:** *A man stands on the steps of a small shingled house on Nevis. Its twin peaks are a typical architectural detail on the English-speaking islands.*

ABOVE: *Friends and family swim in the river that runs behind a house in the hills of Guadeloupe.* **RIGHT:** *Some of the inhabitants of Nevis swim in a sheltered cove.*

LOOKING
OUTSIDE

THE architecture of the Caribbean is a synthesis of different influences. Each island brings to it a unique personality. To the attentive viewer, each island has intrinsic characteristics that distinguish it from the others. As proof of this, it suffices to note the numerous differences between the houses of Guadeloupe and those of Martinique, particularly in the foundations and the rhythms of the façades. And yet these islands have parallel histories. They were colonized by the same nation and the same ethnic groups settled on them. On each island, the same mixture produced different effects and assumed different qualities.

The architectural style developed at the same time as a lifestyle that was specifically Caribbean. The architecture of the Caribbean is first and foremost an architecture for life out-of-doors. Daily activities take place in spaces that are mostly outside the framework of the house itself. And even the framework is open to the outdoors, offering protection only from the sun and the rain.

In the Antilles, houses are sited and domestic activities planned so as to take advantage of the dominant trade *winds—winds that blow constantly from the east to the west, bringing with them a freshness that is indispensable to life on the islands.*

In hot climates, there are many hours when it is more pleasant to be outside than inside. Buildings become a background canvas for a composition in which the garden is as precisely laid out as the house itself. Between these two areas—extra muros and intra muros—the gallery is an organic link, interior and exterior at the same time.

Neither an indoor nor an outdoor space, the gallery or verandah provides a separation between the brightness and heat of the outside world and the coolness and modulated light of the interior. It is not surprising that it is the decorative showplace of the house, an element to be experienced and appreciated from both the exterior and the interior, no matter what the scale of the house to which it belongs.

PRECEDING PAGES: *On St. Barth's, a garden in the popular taste features a pair of cacti in white-polka-dotted pots, a delicate wrought-iron gate, and an arch covered in bougainvillea.*

V I E W S

PRECEDING PAGES: *On Barbados, a terrace provides an uninterrupted view of the ocean as well as a space that is protected from the sun.* **RIGHT:** *A forest of coconut trees separates a house on Nevis from the sea.*

In a valley on Antigua, village houses are nestled in the lush green countryside.

The method of agriculture follows the terrain of the islands. Stone fences delineate the fields on St. Barthélémy.

The view from Clarence House, an official residence for the government of Antigua, is of English Harbour, the former British naval base in the Lesser Antilles.

ABOVE: *A row of coconut palms lines one of the canals on the Waterworks estate, on Montserrat.* **RIGHT:** *Nestled among palm trees, situated by the water, or set atop a hill, the Caribbean house is an intrinsic part of the varied landscape.*

ABOVE: *Small houses are set at the bottom of the hill under a turbulent sky.* **LEFT:** *An abandoned windmill in Les Grands Fonds de Ste. Anne on Guadeloupe is a romantic sight.*

45

A sweeping verandah on Nevis overlooks a lush garden.

ABOVE: *Sugarcane is cut by hand on the gentle slopes near the sea on Martinique.* **LEFT:** *Sea and land are visually tied together in many of the Caribbean islands.* **OVERLEAF:** *Le Diamant, an enormous rock off the coast, is one of Martinique's landmarks.*

C O L O R

ABOVE AND RIGHT: *Hot pink, bright yellow, vibrant turquoise,
and luminescent lilac are some of the colors of island buildings.*
PRECEDING PAGES: *On Guadeloupe, the bright colors and decorative
sunrise motifs create a naive tableau.*

A house on Haiti provides a striking example of the strong and uninhibited graphic designs that are typical of many houses on the island.

ABOVE: *The lacelike delicacy of the balcony railing and the panel over the door contrast the bright blue trim of a Port-au-Prince residence.* **LEFT:** *The yellow-and-red shutters are a counterpoint to the blue walls of this house on Montserrat.* **OVERLEAF:** *Yellow, blue, and red are the palette of this Haitian country house.*

RIGHT: *Shocking pink and pale yellow offer an unusual color combination.* **BELOW:** *The red designs in relief on the verandah gate add a jaunty note to a blue-and-white painted house.*

ABOVE: *Green paint outlines the roof, windows, shutters, and doors of a bright yellow house.*
RIGHT: *The reinforced-concrete walls and corrugated tin roof have been painted in compatible blues and greens.*

Vibrant turquoise with a moss-green trim was chosen for this triple-peaked-roof town house.

The round louvered window below the peak of a pink painted house on Haiti lets air into the attic.

On Haiti, a two-tone pink-and-blue house, with a roof decorated in fretwork, stands as a piece of folk art in a barren landscape.

FAÇADES

ABOVE: *Tall breadfruit trees, part of the long-established garden, frame the entrance to Pécoul, a 1760 sugarcane plantation house on Martinique. The matching openings of the front and back windows allow views through the main building.* **PRECEDING PAGES:** *Pécoul presents a symmetrical façade that is broken only by the kitchen chimney at right.*

BELOW: *The deep sloping roof of the Martinique stone house known as Le Gaoulé is made of local tiles.*

ABOVE: *Zevalos, a tall and elegant building made of prefabricated cast-iron units, rises above the flatlands of Grande-Terre on the island of Guadeloupe.* **RIGHT:** *The use of brick and the wrought-iron balconies of a house in Pointe-à-Pitre are rare on Guadeloupe.*

ABOVE: *The extravagantly peaked roof of a house on Haiti is an example of the fancifulness that is characteristic of many of the structures on the island.*

BELOW: *A profusion of crotons is near the former vegetable garden at the side of Pécoul, on Martinique. A huge stone urn stands on the lawn.* **OVERLEAF:** *La Frégate, with its second floor above the gallery, is typical of Martinican plantation houses.*

The gallery at the Villa Nova Great House on Barbados has crisp white latticework overgrown with plants.

Trellis-shuttered windows are set in the wood-shingled wall of the 1740 L'Hermitage, one of the oldest wooden houses in the Antilles.

In a house in Reading on the island of Jamaica, tall louvered bedroom doors open directly onto the back garden.

Arched windows and curved shutters ornament one of the sides of the Alexandra Hotel in Jacmel, Haiti.

Open or enclosed, made of prefabricated metal or artisan-carved wood, a variety of balconies and verandahs decorate the city and country houses of Montserrat, Guadeloupe, Antigua, and Haiti.

86

ABOVE: *The fanciful fretwork and curved balconies of a private house on Haiti are a new interpretation of the original turn-of-the-century Victorian detailing.* **LEFT:** *Plants in pots punctuate the verandah of Bois Debout, a plantation house on Guadeloupe.*

ABOVE: *A delicate cornice decorates a small corrugated tin–roofed house.* **RIGHT:** *A wood balcony faces the rear courtyard of Maison Nemausat, in Basse-Terre, Guadeloupe.*

ABOVE: *Each of the small build-ings that make up a vacation compound on St. Barth's is topped with a red corrugated-metal roof and trimmed in a decorative border.* **LEFT:** *Set on a hill, the main house of La Pagésie, at Pointe Noire on Guadeloupe, is surrounded by groves of coffee trees.*

The verandah's cutout wood motifs in the shape of fish heads are characteristic on Marie-Galante, an island of fishermen. The sunrise motif is for good luck.

The white-and-pastel-walled 18th-century houses in San Juan, Puerto Rico, feature wood and wrought-iron cantilevered balconies that give the buildings their Spanish look.

A simple wooden bench, painted to match the shutters, stands on the rear gallery of Waterworks, a plantation house on Montserrat.

ABOVE: *In Pointe-à-Pitre, Guadeloupe, wrought-iron balconies decorate the shuttered windows of a city house.* **RIGHT:** *Tall trees shade the front façade of a small inn above Plymouth, on Montserrat, that was a family residence at the turn of the century.*

GARDENS

PRECEDING PAGES: *In a late-19th-century house in Basse-Terre, on Guadeloupe, the ground-floor gallery is planted with large ferns in terra-cotta pots.* **RIGHT:** *Pink flowers provide a touch of color in a garden on Guadeloupe.*

The plants and flowers on the different tropical islands—including lychee trees, **ABOVE RIGHT,** *and huge water lilies,* **ABOVE FAR RIGHT—** *are as colorful as they are lush.*

ABOVE: *The irrigation reservoirs at Bois Debout, an estate located at Basse-Terre on Guadeloupe, were designed to be aesthetic as well as functional.* **LEFT:** *Red draceana bushes frame a shimmering cascade on the grounds of a sugarcane estate known as Pécoul on Martinique.*

An orchid nursery is in back of the garden that surrounds the Villa Nova Great House on Barbados.

*Large terra-cotta jars that were the ballast on cargo ships
transporting meat and oil from Europe to the Lesser Antilles, as*

well as garden ornaments made of terra-cotta, now decorate many Caribbean gardens and gateways.

RIGHT: *An old marble bathtub has been planted with water lilies.* **BELOW AND TOP FAR RIGHT:** *Spectacular pink blossoms and giant crotons are some of the striking features of a garden on Martinique.*

LEFT: *Curved stone benches are set among the trees as a shady resting spot in a garden on Barbados.*

111

The pale colors of the trim complement the luxuriant garden.

In the Caribbean, trees are always green, and only a few flowers and fruits have distinct seasons. An asparagus fern has grown to gigantic proportions, **ABOVE RIGHT.**

The traveler's-tree, **ABOVE LEFT,** *collects water at the base of its leaves; the waterwheel that stands at the end of the canal on an estate on Guadeloupe adds a picturesque touch,* **ABOVE RIGHT.**

Because the plantation house of Beauséjour is situated on the north coast of Martinique, which is the most humid part of the island, the garden surrounding the house is particularly luxuriant.

On Nevis, the garden of the
Montpelier estate, an old
plantation house that is now
a hotel, offers a play of light
and shade. Huge specimens
of ficus grow over the wide
steps of volcanic stone.

A small corner of a garden on Martinique is used as a nursery for potted orchids.

Huge bushes with vibrantly colored flowers grow near the main house of an estate on Guadeloupe.

Vacation houses on St. Barth's are linked by planked walkways lined with plants.

LOOKING INSIDE

TODAY'S *West Indian houses are amalgams of scholarly architecture on the one hand and on the other the architecture of the countrysides of both Europe and Africa. Thus within one luxurious house can be found windows ordered in a totally Palladian manner and doors closed with wooden latches based on African designs.*

The house and its surroundings, the furniture, and the garden reflect the Caribbean sensibility and the order of society. Thus the expressly desired discomfort of the sofa on which one sits while waiting to be received by the master of the house; the whispers and mumbling voices that can be heard through thin wooden partitions; the sensuality of exotic veined woods, richly scented, warm in tone. All are part of a decor that hides and reveals at the same time— the shutters that shield an inquisitive stare; the row of doors that let in light and that sometimes frame a momentary scene uncovered in passing.

Perhaps in memory of the slave whose cabin was a refuge for privacy, West Indians declare their love for their homes with the delicate frills and lacework that adorn galleries and interiors. Large plantation houses, the most imposing residences in the Antilles, are set on the highest ground, from which they dominate the landscape and profit from the winds. In the 18th century, galleries and verandahs suitable to the climate gave the great European-inspired houses an essential Creole characteristic.

In the towns, which are hot and sheltered from the wind, the typical house sits on a narrow street and usually includes a store or warehouse on the street level.

The popular Caribbean house, or case, *is usually a rural dwelling. For many Antilleans who have traditionally owned little else, the house is the object of a special affection. That explains the care and attention lavished on these modest buildings, from the imagination shown in each uniquely decorated exterior to the pride reflected in the well-arranged furniture and mementos inside.*

PRECEDING PAGES: *A wood composition depicting a bowl filled with fruit has been cut out and applied to the paneled wall of a dining room on Jamaica.*

LIVING

ABOVE: *Louvered panels are used as interior partitions to divide the sitting room on the estate of Good Hope on Jamaica.*
PRECEDING PAGES: *At Parham Hill, a plantation house on Antigua, the plank wood floor in the office, where workers came to collect their wages, has been stained red to match the walls.*

BELOW: *A barometer hangs on the wall of the formal living room of the Good Hope Great House. A large dog lies on the cool floor that has been polished to a mirrorlike finish.*

RIGHT: *In the sitting room of Le Maud'Huy, an 1873 plantation house on the east coast of Guadeloupe, two rocking chairs are pulled up to a small table on which are displayed bottles filled with the customary rum punch.*

OVERLEAF: *The spacious gallery at La Frégate on Martinique has been furnished with comfortable chairs and functions as a living room.*

Pécoul, on Martinique, is an estate that has remained in the same family since its beginnings in the mid-18th century. Ancestral portraits welcome visitors to the house.

ABOVE: *The rocking chair on a tiled porch on Guadeloupe provides a shady and inviting place to enjoy the cool evening air.* **RIGHT:** *The rocking chairs and a small table in the living room of a suburban house in St. Claude, on Guadeloupe, were crafted in the Caribbean. An antique gramophone is positioned in the corner by the door.*

A carved wood panel that illustrates an underwater scene covers one wall in the dining room of a vacation house on Jamaica.

The louvered living room window is draped with green cotton. Shiny ceramic tile covers the floor.

The wall sconce in a Jamaican dining room has been carved in a pineapple motif.

An imitation bamboo storage unit with pull-out wicker drawers and bronze-colored hardware stands in front of a bedroom window on Jamaica. Frangipani blossoms fill a green vase.

Three arches bisect the living room of Parham Hill, a 1722 plantation house on Antigua. The ornate architectural details, painted in white, contrast with the dark green of the walls.

RIGHT: *The walls, floor, and furniture in the living room at Waterworks, a plantation house on Montserrat, are all of dark wood.* **OVERLEAF:** *The front gallery of the 1760 plantation house known as Pécoul, on Martinique, functions as a living room. The ocher and turquoise hues, which are reminiscent of 18th-century French interiors, contrast with the softer variegated colors of the tile floor.*

150

LEFT AND BELOW: *Brass chandeliers hang from the high ceiling in the formal sitting room of a house in Port-au-Prince, Haiti. A series of arched doorways acts as a partition between the main reception rooms.* **OVERLEAF:** *In Basse-Terre, Guadeloupe, the living room of an antiques-filled house takes up the entire ground floor.*

154

In the main living room of Clarence House, an official residence on Antigua, a portrait of Queen Elizabeth and Prince Philip hangs between two windows and above a desk and chair.

ABOVE LEFT: *The soft turquoise frame of the Haitian rocking chair harmonizes with the early-20th-century tile floor.* **ABOVE RIGHT:** *In the hall of a converted town house in Jacmel, Haiti, hangs a contemporary pen-and-ink sketch of the façade of the hotel.*

ABOVE LEFT: *A few hats, a bag, an umbrella, and canes hang on a rack in the gallery of a house on Guadeloupe.* **ABOVE RIGHT:** *A high-legged mahogany console, one of the rare pieces of furniture that are of pure Martinican origin, was designed as a stand-up desk.*

An assortment of typically Caribbean rockers furnishes the living room of Le Maud' Huy, a plantation house on Guadeloupe that was built in 1873 by August Pauvert, the director of the sugarcane factory in a nearby village.

In a house known as L'Hermitage, on the island of Nevis, a water-color hangs in the corner of the ground-floor bedroom; an oil lamp recalls the time when the house lacked electricity; mangoes sit on

the verandah table; and dried pieces of coral are displayed on a stand that was used for holding water jars.

RIGHT: *The main sitting room in one of the oldest houses in the Caribbean, the mid-17th-century St. Nicholas Abbey on Barbados, has been furnished with a variety of rockers and chairs.* **OVERLEAF:** *At the bottom of the mahogany staircase at Le Maud'Huy on Guadeloupe stands a planter's chair. The master of the house would rest his legs on the long swing-out arms while a servant removed his boots.*

ABOVE: *Antique dolls occupy some of the chairs in the brilliant blue living room at the Alexandra Hotel on Haiti.* **RIGHT:** *At the entrance to the covered gallery at La Frégate, on Martinique, rustic chairs recall the feeling of a French country house.*

DINING

ABOVE: *A doorway frames the view into the formal dining room of the 1750 Governor's House on Montserrat.* **LEFT:** *At the rear of a house in Port-au-Prince, Haiti, two doorways separate the dining room from the terrace. On the table is a bouquet of anthurium.* **PRECEDING PAGES:** *Glass hurricane lamps stand on the dining table at Parham Hill on Antigua. The vermilion-colored walls add to the elegance of the room.*

In St. Nicholas Abbey on Barbados, the formal dining room has been situated to receive the afternoon sun. The walls are paneled.

ABOVE LEFT AND ABOVE RIGHT: *Crystal glasses and silver serving pieces sparkle on a rolling cart in the green-walled dining room at Waterworks, on Montserrat.*

174

ABOVE LEFT: *The intimate family dining room at La Frégate, on Martinique, is furnished with white painted furniture.* **ABOVE RIGHT:** *The butterfly-shaped chair backs in a popular house at Anse Bertrand on Guadeloupe are the local artisan's signature.*

176

LEFT: *At L'Hermitage, a 1740 wood-shingled house on Nevis, the combination living and dining room is situated in the oldest part of the house.*
OVERLEAF: *The informal dining room of the Good Hope Great House has been furnished with English-style mahogany furniture hand-crafted on Jamaica.*

At Pécoul, on Martinique, the centrally placed main room of the house is used for dining. The mahogany dining table and console contrast with the unglazed tile floors, red slat-back chairs, and yellow walls.

The formal dining room at Le Maud'Huy, on Guadeloupe, features a huge oval table of polished mahogany. Hurricane lamps replace the more usual candlesticks.

ABOVE: *A system of screenlike louvered partitions stands at one end of the large dining room of Antigua's Weatherhills estate.* **LEFT:** *A wall-hung china rack holds a collection of flea-market finds in the green-walled dining room of Maison Nemausat, on Guadeloupe.*

RIGHT: *The space that functions as the main living area in a popular house in Grand Fonds, on Martinique, has been painted pink and green.* **BELOW:** *At Pécoul, on Martinique, the mahogany dining table is surrounded by red slat-backed chairs. The floor is unglazed tile.*

The wood plank walls of the dining room of the Charlotte Inn, in Lucea on the north coast of Jamaica, have been painted royal blue. A mahogany console stands against one wall. The tables are surrounded by English Chippendale-style chairs.

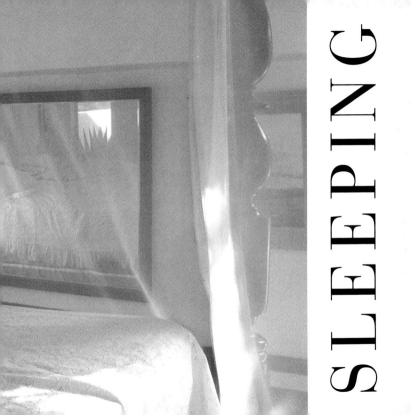

SLEEPING

ABOVE AND RIGHT: *The carved mahogany pineapple and twisted rope detailing on the four-poster canopy beds is typically Jamaican.*
PRECEDING PAGES: *The white gauze mosquito netting contributes to the dreamlike quality of a bedroom on St. Barthélémy.*

A chaise with a double shell–shaped base sits under the windows facing the ocean in the master bedroom of the late-18th-century Rose Hall Great House in Jamaica.

The uprights of the high four-poster bed in one of the bedrooms at L'Hermitage, on Nevis, are thin and graceful. The stool facilitates climbing into bed.

ABOVE AND LEFT: *Mahogany is the wood used for the frames and carved posts of many beds in the Caribbean. The mosquito netting and white bedclothes contrast with the dark wood.* **OVERLEAF:** *Yards of mosquito netting hang above the two double four-poster beds at Pécoul, on Martinique.*

One of the bedrooms in the Charlotte Inn in Lucea, Jamaica, has an old-fashioned bathtub in the room, merely partitioned off with a plastic lace-patterned curtain.

ABOVE LEFT: *An iron bed and a chest for a baby's layette furnish a bedroom on Guadeloupe.* **ABOVE RIGHT:** *The mahogany bed is a Guadaloupian variation of the standard four-poster.*

ABOVE LEFT: *The pale green color scheme contributes to the serenity of the bedroom on Antigua.* **ABOVE RIGHT:** *Mosquito netting is tied above an iron bed in a blue-walled bedroom on Guadeloupe.*

ABOVE: *A four-poster bed swathed in mosquito netting is in a simply furnished St. Barth's guest room.* **LEFT:** *One of the bedrooms in St. Nicholas Abbey is furnished with an ornate 19th-century English bed.*

A LITTLE STYLE BOOK

ENGLISH STYLE

SUZANNE SLESIN
STAFFORD CLIFF
PHOTOGRAPHS BY
KEN KIRKWOOD

A LITTLE STYLE BOOK

FRENCH STYLE

SUZANNE SLESIN
STAFFORD CLIFF
PHOTOGRAPHS BY
JACQUES DIRAND

A LITTLE STYLE BOOK

JAPANESE STYLE

SUZANNE SLESIN
STAFFORD CLIFF
DANIEL ROZENSZTROCH
PHOTOGRAPHS BY
GILLES DE CHABANEIX

Other titles in the series

THE ALEXANDER SHAKESPEARE

General Editor
R.B. Kennedy

Additional notes and editing
Mike Gould

KING LEAR

William Shakespeare

COLLINS
CLASSICS

Harper Press
An imprint of HarperCollins*Publishers*
77–85 Fulham Palace Road
Hammersmith
London W6 8JB

This Harper Press paperback edition published 2011

A catalogue record for this book is available from the British Library

ISBN-13: 978-0-00-790233-0

Printed and bound in Great Britain by Clays Ltd, St Ives plc

MIX
Paper from
responsible sources
FSC® C007454

FSC™ is a non-profit international organisation established to promote
the responsible management of the world's forests. Products carrying the
FSC label are independently certified to assure consumers that they come
from forests that are managed to meet the social, economic and
ecological needs of present and future generations,
and other controlled sources.

Find out more about HarperCollins and the environment at
www.harpercollins.co.uk/green

Life & Times section © Gerard Cheshire
Introduction by Philip Hobsbaum
Shakespeare: Words and Phrases adapted from
Collins English Dictionary
Typesetting in Kalix by Palimpsest Book Production Limited,
Falkirk, Stirlingshire

3

Prefatory Note

This Shakespeare play uses the full Alexander text. By keeping in mind the fact that the language has changed considerably in four hundred years, as have customs, jokes, and stage conventions, the editors have aimed at helping the modern reader – whether English is their mother tongue or not – to grasp the full significance of the play. The Notes, intended primarily for examination candidates, are presented in a simple, direct style. The needs of those unfamiliar with British culture have been specially considered.

Since quiet study of the printed word is unlikely to bring fully to life plays that were written directly for the public theatre, attention has been drawn to dramatic effects which are important in performance. The editors see Shakespeare's plays as living works of art which can be enjoyed today on stage, film and television in many parts of the world.

CONTENTS

An Elizabethan playhouse. Note the apron stage protruding into the auditorium, the space below it, the inner room at the rear of the stage, the gallery above the inner stage, the canopy over the main stage, and the absence of a roof over the audience.

The Theatre in Shakespeare's Day

On the face of it, the conditions in the Elizabethan theatre were not such as to encourage great writers. The public playhouse itself was not very different from an ordinary inn-yard; it was open to the weather; among the spectators were often louts, pickpockets and prostitutes; some of the actors played up to the rowdy elements in the audience by inserting their own jokes into the authors' lines, while others spoke their words loudly but unfeelingly; the presentation was often rough and noisy, with fireworks to represent storms and battles, and a table and a few chairs to represent a tavern; there were no actresses, so boys took the parts of women, even such subtle and mature ones as Cleopatra and Lady Macbeth; there was rarely any scenery at all in the modern sense. In fact, a quick inspection of the English theatre in the reign of Elizabeth I by a time-traveller from the twentieth century might well produce only one positive reaction: the costumes were often elaborate and beautiful.

Shakespeare himself makes frequent comments in his plays about the limitations of the playhouse and the actors of his time, often apologizing for them. At the beginning of *Henry V* the Prologue refers to the stage as 'this unworthy scaffold' and to the theatre building (the Globe, probably) as 'this wooden O', and emphasizes the urgent need for imagination in making up for all the deficiencies of presentation. In introducing Act IV the Chorus goes so far as to say:

> . . . we shall much disgrace
> With four or five most vile and ragged foils,
> Right ill-dispos'd in brawl ridiculous,
> The name of Agincourt, (lines 49–52)

In *A Midsummer Night's Dream* (Act V, Scene i) he seems to dismiss actors with the words:

The best in this kind are but shadows.

Yet Elizabeth's theatre, with all its faults, stimulated dramatists to a variety of achievement that has never been equalled and, in Shakespeare, produced one of the greatest writers in history. In spite of all his grumbles he seems to have been fascinated by the challenge that it presented him with. It is necessary to re-examine his theatre carefully in order to understand how he was able to achieve so much with the materials he chose to use. What sort of place was the Elizabethan playhouse in reality? What sort of people were these criticized actors? And what sort of audiences gave them their living?

The Development of the Theatre up to Shakespeare's Time

For centuries in England noblemen had employed groups of skilled people to entertain them when required. Under Tudor rule, as England became more secure and united, actors such as these were given more freedom, and they often performed in public, while still acknowledging their 'overlords' (in the 1570s, for example, when Shakespeare was still a schoolboy at Stratford, one famous company was called 'Lord Leicester's Men'). London was rapidly becoming larger and more important in the second half of the sixteenth century, and many of the companies of actors took the opportunities offered to establish themselves at inns on the main roads leading to the City (for example, the Boar's Head in Whitechapel and the Tabard in South-wark) or in the City itself. These groups of actors would come to an agreement with the inn-keeper which would give them the use of the yard for their performances after people had eaten and drunk well in the middle of the day. Before long, some inns were taken over completely by companies of players and thus became the first public theatres. In 1574 the officials of the City of London issued an order which shows clearly that these theatres were both popular and also offensive to some respectable people, because the order complains about 'the inordinate haunting of great multitudes of people, specially youth, to plays interludes and shows; namely occasion of frays and quarrels, evil practices of incontinency in great inns . . .' There is evidence that, on public holidays, the theatres on the banks of the Thames were crowded with noisy apprentices and tradesmen, but it would be wrong to think that audiences were always undiscriminating and loudmouthed. In spite of the disapproval of Puritans and the more staid members of society, by the 1590s, when Shakespeare's plays were beginning to be performed, audiences consisted of a good cross-section of English society, nobility as well as workers, intellectuals as well as simple people out for a laugh; also (and in this respect English theatres were unique in Europe), it was quite normal for respectable women to attend plays. So Shakespeare had to write plays which would appeal to people of widely different kinds. He had to provide 'something for everyone' but at the same time to take care to unify the material so that it would not seem to fall into separate pieces as they watched it. A speech like that of the drunken porter in *Macbeth* could provide the 'groundlings' with a belly-laugh, but also held a deeper significance for those who could appreciate it. The audience he wrote for was one of a number of apparent drawbacks which Shakespeare was able to turn to his and our advantage.

Shakespeare's Actors

Nor were all the actors of the time mere 'rogues, vagabonds and sturdy beggars' as some were described in a Statute of 1572. It is true that many of them had a hard life and earned very little money, but leading actors could become partners in the ownership of the theatres in which they acted: Shakespeare was a shareholder in the Globe and the Blackfriars theatres when he was an actor as well as a playwright. In any case, the attacks made on Elizabethan actors were usually directed at their morals and not at their acting ability; it is clear that many of them must have been good at their trade if they were able to interpret complex works like the great tragedies in such a way as to attract enthusiastic audiences. Undoubtedly some of the boys took the women's parts with skill and confidence, since a man called Coryate, visiting Venice in 1611, expressed surprise that women could act as well as they: 'I saw women act, a thing that I never saw before . . . and they performed it with as good a grace, action, gesture . . . as ever I saw any masculine actor.' The quality of most of the actors who first presented Shakespeare's plays is probably accurately summed up by Fynes Moryson, who wrote, '. . . as there be, in my opinion, more plays in London than in all the parts of the world I have seen, so do these players or comedians excel all other in the world.'

The Structure of the Public Theatre

Although the 'purpose-built' theatres were based on the inn-yards which had been used for play-acting, most of them were circular. The walls contained galleries on three storeys from which the wealthier patrons watched, they must have been something like the 'boxes' in a modern theatre, except that they held much larger numbers – as many as 1500. The 'groundlings' stood on the floor of the building, facing a raised stage which projected from the 'stage-wall', the main features of which were:

1 a small room opening on to the back of the main stage and on the same level as it (rear stage),
2 a gallery above this inner stage (upper stage),
3 canopy projecting from above the gallery over the main stage, to protect the actors from the weather (the 700 or 800 members of the audience who occupied the yard, or 'pit' as we call it today, had the sky above them).

In addition to these features there were dressing-rooms behind the stage and a space underneath it from which entrances could be made through trap-doors. All the acting areas – main stage, rear stage, upper stage and under stage – could be entered by actors directly from their dressing rooms, and all of them were used in productions of Shakespeare's plays. For example, the inner stage, an almost cavelike structure, would have been where Ferdinand and Miranda are 'discovered' playing chess in the last act of *The Tempest*, while the upper stage was certainly the balcony from which Romeo climbs down in Act III of *Romeo and Juliet*.

It can be seen that such a building, simple but adaptable, was not really unsuited to the presentation of plays like Shakespeare's. On the contrary, its simplicity guaranteed the minimum of distraction, while its shape and construction must have produced a sense of involvement on the part of the audience that modern producers would envy.

Other Resources of the Elizabethan Theatre

Although there were few attempts at scenery in the public theatre (painted backcloths were occasionally used in court performances), Shakespeare and his fellow playwrights were able to make use of a fair variety of 'properties', lists of such articles have survived: they include beds, tables, thrones, and also trees, walls, a gallows, a Trojan horse and a 'Mouth of Hell'; in a list of properties belonging to the manager, Philip Henslowe, the curious item 'two mossy banks' appears. Possibly one of them was used for the

> bank whereon the wild thyme blows,
> Where oxlips and the nodding violet grows

in *A Midsummer Night's Dream* (Act II, Scene i). Once again, imagination must have been required of the audience.

Costumes were the one aspect of stage production in which

trouble and expense were hardly ever spared to obtain a magnificent effect. Only occasionally did they attempt any historical accuracy (almost all Elizabethan productions were what we should call 'modern-dress' ones), but they were appropriate to the characters who wore them: kings were seen to be kings and beggars were similarly unmistakable. It is an odd fact that there was usually no attempt at illusion in the costuming: if a costume looked fine and rich it probably was. Indeed, some of the costumes were almost unbelievably expensive. Henslowe lent his company £19 to buy a cloak, and the Alleyn brothers, well-known actors, gave £20 for a 'black velvet cloak, with sleeves embroidered all with silver and gold, lined with black satin striped with gold'.

With the one exception of the costumes, the 'machinery' of the playhouse was economical and uncomplicated rather than crude and rough, as we can see from this second and more leisurely look at it. This meant that playwrights were stimulated to produce the imaginative effects that they wanted from the language that they used. In the case of a really great writer like Shakespeare, when he had learned his trade in the theatre as an actor, it seems that he received quite enough assistance of a mechanical and structural kind without having irksome restrictions and conventions imposed on him; it is interesting to try to guess what he would have done with the highly complex apparatus of a modern television studio. We can see when we look back to his time that he used his instrument, the Elizabethan theatre, to the full, but placed his ultimate reliance on the communication between his imagination and that of his audience through the medium of words. It is, above all, his rich and wonderful use of language that must have made play-going at that time a memorable experience for people of widely different kinds. Fortunately, the deep satisfaction of appreciating and enjoying Shakespeare's work can be ours also, if we are willing to overcome the language difficulty produced by the passing of time.

Shakespeare: A Timeline

Very little indeed is known about Shakespeare's private life; the facts included here are almost the only indisputable ones. The dates of Shakespeare's plays are those on which they were first produced.

1558	Queen Elizabeth crowned.
1561	Francis Bacon born.
1564	Christopher Marlowe born.

William Shakespeare born, April 23rd, baptized April 26th.

1566

Shakespeare's brother, Gilbert, born.

1567 Mary, Queen of Scots, deposed.
James VI (later James I of England) crowned King of Scotland.

1572 Ben Jonson born.
Lord Leicester's Company (of players) licensed; later called Lord Strange's, then the Lord Chamberlain's and finally (under James) the King's Men.

1573 John Donne born.

1574 The Common Council of London directs that all plays and playhouses in London must be licensed.

1576 James Burbage builds the first public playhouse, The Theatre, at Shoreditch, outside the walls of the City.

1577 Francis Drake begins his voyage round the world (completed 1580).
Holinshed's Chronicles of England, Scotland and Ireland published (which

Shakespeare later used
extensively).

1582		Shakespeare married to Anne Hathaway.
1583	The Queen's Company founded by royal warrant.	Shakespeare's daughter, Susanna, born.
1585		Shakespeare's twins, Hamnet and Judith, born.
1586	Sir Philip Sidney, the Elizabethan ideal 'Christian knight', poet, patron, soldier, killed at Zutphen in the Low Countries.	
1587	Mary, Queen of Scots, beheaded. Marlowe's *Tamburlaine (Part I)* first staged.	
1588	Defeat of the Spanish Armada. Marlowe's *Tamburlaine (Part II)* first staged.	
1589	Marlowe's *Jew of Malta* and Kyd's *Spanish Tragedy* (a 'revenge tragedy' and one of the most popular plays of Elizabethan times).	
1590	Spenser's *Faerie Queene* (Books I–III) published.	
1592	Marlowe's *Doctor Faustus* and *Edward II* first staged. Witchcraft trials in Scotland. Robert Greene, a rival playwright, refers to Shakespeare as 'an upstart crow' and 'the only Shake-scene in a country'.	*Titus Andronicus* *Henry VI, Parts I, II and III* *Richard III*
1593	London theatres closed by the plague. Christopher Marlowe killed in a Deptford tavern.	*Two Gentlemen of Verona* *Comedy of Errors* *The Taming of the Shrew* *Love's Labour's Lost*
1594	Shakespeare's company becomes The Lord Chamberlain's Men.	*Romeo and Juliet*

1595	Raleigh's first expedition to Guiana. Last expedition of Drake and Hawkins (both died).	*Richard II* *A Midsummer Night's Dream*
1596	Spenser's *Faerie Queene* (Books IV–VI) published. James Burbage buys rooms at Blackfriars and begins to convert them into a theatre.	*King John* *The Merchant of Venice* Shakespeare's son Hamnet dies. Shakespeare's father is granted a coat of arms.
1597	James Burbage dies, his son Richard, a famous actor, turns the Blackfriars Theatre into a private playhouse.	*Henry IV (Part I)* Shakespeare buys and redecorates New Place at Stratford.
1598	Death of Philip II of Spain	*Henry IV (Part II)* *Much Ado About Nothing*
1599	Death of Edmund Spenser. The Globe Theatre completed at Bankside by Richard and Cuthbert Burbage.	*Henry V* *Julius Caesar* *As You Like It*
1600	Fortune Theatre built at Cripplegate. East India Company founded for the extension of English trade and influence in the East. The Children of the Chapel begin to use the hall at Blackfriars.	*Merry Wives of Windsor* *Troilus and Cressida*
1601		*Hamlet*
1602	Sir Thomas Bodley's library opened at Oxford.	*Twelfth Night*
1603	Death of Queen Elizabeth. James I comes to the throne. Shakespeare's company becomes The King's Men. Raleigh tried, condemned and sent to the Tower	
1604	Treaty of peace with Spain	*Measure for Measure* *Othello* *All's Well that Ends Well*
1605	The Gunpowder Plot: an attempt by a group of Catholics to blow up the Houses of Parliament.	

1606	Guy Fawkes and other plotters executed.	*Macbeth* *King Lear*
1607	Virginia, in America, colonized. A great frost in England.	*Antony and Cleopatra* *Timon of Athens* *Coriolanus* Shakespeare's daughter, Susanna, married to Dr. John Hall.
1608	The company of the Children of the Chapel Royal (who had performed at Blackfriars for ten years) is disbanded. John Milton born. Notorious pirates executed in London.	Richard Burbage leases the Blackfriars Theatre to six of his fellow actors, including Shakespeare. *Pericles, Prince of Tyre*
1609		Shakespeare's Sonnets published.
1610	A great drought in England	*Cymbeline*
1611	Chapman completes his great translation of the *Iliad*, the story of Troy. Authorized Version of the Bible published.	*A Winter's Tale* *The Tempest*
1612	Webster's *The White Devil* first staged.	Shakespeare's brother, Gilbert, dies.
1613	Globe theatre burnt down during a performance of *Henry VIII* (the firing of small cannon set fire to the thatched roof). Webster's *Duchess of Malfi* first staged.	*Henry VIII* *Two Noble Kinsmen* Shakespeare buys a house at Blackfriars.
1614	Globe Theatre rebuilt in 'far finer manner than before'.	
1616	Ben Jonson publishes his plays in one volume. Raleigh released from the Tower in order to prepare an expedition to the gold mines of Guiana.	Shakespeare's daughter, Judith, marries Thomas Quiney. Death of Shakespeare on his birthday, April 23rd.
1618	Raleigh returns to England and is executed on the charge for which he was imprisoned in 1603.	
1623	Publication of the Folio edition of Shakespeare's plays	Death of Anne Shakespeare (née Hathaway).

Life & Times

William Shakespeare the Playwright

There exists a curious paradox when it comes to the life of William Shakespeare. He easily has more words written about him than any other famous English writer, yet we know the least about him. This inevitably means that most of what is written about him is either fabrication or speculation. The reason why so little is known about Shakespeare is that he wasn't a novelist or a historian or a man of letters. He was a playwright, and playwrights were considered fairly low on the social pecking order in Elizabethan society. Writing plays was about providing entertainment for the masses – the great unwashed. It was the equivalent to being a journalist for a tabloid newspaper.

In fact, we only know of Shakespeare's work because two of his friends had the foresight to collect his plays together following his death and have them printed. The only reason they did so was apparently because they rated his talent and thought it would be a shame if his words were lost.

Consequently his body of work has ever since been assessed and reassessed as the greatest contribution to English literature. That is despite the fact that we know that different printers took it upon themselves to heavily edit the material they worked from. We also know that Elizabethan plays were worked and reworked frequently, so that they evolved over time until they were honed to perfection, which means that many different hands played their part in the active writing process. It would therefore be fair to say that any play attributed to Shakespeare is unlikely to contain a great deal of original input. Even the plots were based on well known historical events, so it would be hard to know what fragments of any Shakespeare play came from that single mind.

One might draw a comparison with the Christian bible, which remains such a compelling read because it came from the collaboration of many contributors and translators over centuries, who each adjusted the stories until they could no longer be improved. As virtually nothing is known of Shakespeare's life and even less about his method of working, we shall never know the truth about his plays. They certainly contain some very elegant phrasing, clever plot devices and plenty of words never before seen in print, but as to whether Shakespeare invented them from a unique imagination or whether he simply took them from others around him is anyone's guess.

The best bet seems to be that Shakespeare probably took the lead role in devising the original drafts of the plays, but was open to collaboration from any source when it came to developing them into workable scripts for effective performances. He would have had to work closely with his fellow actors in rehearsals, thereby finding out where to edit, abridge, alter, reword and so on.

In turn, similar adjustments would have occurred in his absence, so that definitive versions of his plays never really existed. In effect Shakespeare was only responsible for providing the framework of plays, upon which others took liberties over time. This wasn't helped by the fact that the English language itself was not definitive at that time either. The consequence was that people took it upon themselves to spell words however they pleased or to completely change words and phrasing to suit their own preferences.

It is easy to see then, that Shakespeare's plays were always going to have lives of their own, mutating and distorting in detail like Chinese whispers. The culture of creative preservation was simply not established in Elizabethan England. Creative ownership of Shakespeare's plays was lost to him as soon as he released them into the consciousness of others. They saw nothing wrong with taking his ideas and running with them, because no one had ever suggested that one shouldn't, and Shakespeare probably regarded his work in the same way. His plays weren't sacrosanct works of art, they were templates for theatre folk to make their livings from, so they had every right to mould them into productions that drew in the crowds as effectively as possible. Shakespeare was like the helmsman of a sailing ship, steering the vessel but wholly reliant on the team work of his crew to arrive at the desired destination.

It seems that Shakespeare certainly had a natural gift, but the genius of his plays may be attributable to the collective efforts of Shakespeare and others. It is a rather satisfying notion to think that *his* plays might actually be the creative outpourings of the Elizabethan milieu in which Shakespeare immersed himself. That makes them important social documents as well as seminal works of the English language.

Money in Shakespeare's Day

It is extremely difficult, if not impossible, to relate the value of money in our time to its value in another age and to compare prices of commodities today and in the past. Many items *are* simply not comparable on grounds of quality or serviceability.

There was a bewildering variety of coins in use in Elizabethan England. As nearly all English and European coins were gold or silver, they had intrinsic value apart from their official value. This meant that foreign coins circulated freely in England and were officially recognized, for example the French crown (écu) worth about 30p (72 cents), and the Spanish ducat worth about 33p (79 cents). The following table shows some of the coins mentioned by Shakespeare and their relation to one another.

GOLD	British	American	SILVER	British	American
sovereign (heavy type)	£1.50	$3.60	shilling	10p	24c
sovereign (light type)	66p–£1	$1.58–$2.40	groat	1.5p	4c
angel royal	33p–50p	79c–$1.20			
noble	50p	$1.20			
crown	25p	60c			

A comparison of the following prices in Shakespeare's time with the prices of the same items today will give some idea of the change in the value of money.

ITEM	PRICE British	American	ITEM	PRICE British	American
beef, per lb.	0.5p	1c	cherries (lb.)	1p	2c
mutton, leg	7.5p	18c	7 oranges	1p	2c
rabbit	3.5p	9c	1 lemon	1p	2c
chicken	3p	8c	cream (quart)	2.5p	6c
potatoes (lb)	10p	24c	sugar (lb.)	£1	$2.40
carrots (bunch)	1p	2c	sack (wine) (gallon)	14p	34c
8 artichokes	4p	9c	tobacco (oz.)	25p	60c
1 cucumber	1p	2c	biscuits (lb.)	12.5p	30c

INTRODUCTION

The basic plot of *King Lear* is something like a fairy story. It tells of an old man who casts out his younger daughter and splits his kingdom between the elder two. Summarised in this fashion, the plot can be seen to relate to that of *Cinderella*, a theme that has haunted the human consciousness for hundreds of years.

King Lear, therefore, has its predecessors. There are several versions of the story in medieval chronicles, always involving an old king giving away his domains and then being subject to his unworthy elder daughters. What may have sparked off the intensity of Shakespeare's treatment was the case of an elderly courtier, Sir Bryan Annesley, who was declared insane by an elder daughter, Lady Wildgose, while his youngest daughter petitioned King James VI and I for the restitution of the estate. What seems eerie is that the name of this youngest daughter was Cordell.

The story of King Lear was well known in the sixteenth century, and Sir Bryan must have named his faithful girl after a legendary creature without realising, of course, that she would grow up to fulfil the legend. The poignancy of the play itself to no small extent depends upon the way it reflects the conflicts that beset us in life. Lear addresses a question to his three daughters in the first scene, 'Which of you shall we say doth love us most?'. Such a question cannot be decently answered. Love cannot be quantified or elicited. That foolish question leads to grave disorder in the realm and to the destruction of Lear and his family. It is mirrored in the sub-plot, where another aged father casts out a virtuous son and is pilloried by one that is unworthy.

Lear descends through inexorable stages. Throughout the drama he is stripped piece by piece of his lands, possessions and followers. By Act 3 he is found raving in a storm, half-naked - 'Off, off, you lendings!' - entering a hovel in company with a feigned madman and a genuine fool. Lear has been reduced to the basic state of 'a poor, bare, forked animal'. This is in order to educate him into a realisation that other people matter as well as himself.

The education of King Lear proves to be an expensive business. The death of Cordelia at the end transpires with the irrationality of a tragic accident. In the chronicles, she survives; in the play, she is eliminated. There can be no greater *coup de théâtre* than that moment when Albany utters the pious hope, 'The gods defend her', just as Lear enters with his youngest daughter dead in his arms.

The death of Cordelia used often to be questioned, particularly in the eighteenth century. One interpretation could be that Lear stands for the obdurate sinner and that Cordelia, as her name would imply, represents the saint or intercessor who has been sent to save him. Those who have mourned the demise of a young colleague may ponder the import of the apparently unnecessary death of Cordelia. Those who have sat by the bedside of an aged relative may gauge the meaning of Lear's own death: 'Vex not his ghost. O let him pass! He hates him/That would upon the rack of this tough world/Stretch him out longer'.

Lear has been purged by his madness and dies with a kind of hard-won innocence, thinking that he will be at last conjoined with his daughter. Over her prostrate body he seems to receive a revelation to which those others on stage are not parties: 'Look on her. Look, her lips./ Look there, look there!'. The key would appear to be the fifteenth verse of the tenth chapter of Luke's Gospel: 'Whoever shall not receive the kingdom of God as a little child, he shall not enter therein'.

LIST OF CHARACTERS

Lear   King of Britain
King of France
Duke of Burgundy
Duke of Cornwall
Duke of Albany
Earl of Kent
Ear of Gloucester
Edgar   son to Gloucester
Edmund   bastard son to Gloucester
Curan   a courier
Old Man   tenant to Gloucester
Doctor
Fool
Oswald   steward to Goneril
A Captain employed by Edmund
Gentleman attendant on Cordelia
A Herald
Servants to Cornwall
Goneril, Regan, Cordelia daughters to Lear
Knights attending on Lear, Officers, Messengers, Soldiers, and Attendants.

The Scene: Britain

ACT ONE
Scene I

King Lear's palace.

[*Enter* KENT, GLOUCESTER, *and* EDMUND]

Kent

I thought the King had more affected the Duke
of Albany than Cornwall.

Gloucester

It did always seem so to us; but now, in the division of the kingdom, it appears not which of the
Dukes he values most; for equalities are so weigh'd
that curiosity in neither can make choice of
either's moiety.   6

Kent

Is not this your son, my lord?

Gloucester

His breeding, sir, hath been at my charge. I have
so often blush'd to acknowledge him that now I
am braz'd to't.   10

Kent

I cannot conceive you.

Gloucester

Sir, this young fellow's mother could; whereupon
she grew round-womb'd, and had indeed, sir, a
son for her cradle ere she had a husband for her
bed. Do you smell a fault?   15

Kent

I cannot wish the fault undone, the issue of it
being so proper.

Gloucester

But I have a son, sir, by order of law, some year
elder than this, who yet is no dearer in my
account. Though this knave came something
saucily to the world before he was sent for, yet
was his mother fair; there was good sport at his

making, and the whoreson must be acknowl-
edged. – Do you know this noble gentleman,
Edmund?

Edmund

25   No, my lord.

Gloucester

My Lord of Kent. Remember him hereafter as my
honourable friend.

Edmund

My services to your lordship.

Kent

I must love you, and sue to know you better.

Edmund

30   Sir, I shall study deserving.

Gloucester

He hath been out nine years, and away he shall
again. *[Sennet]* The King is coming.

[Enter One bearing a coronet; then LEAR, *then the* DUKES OF
ALBANY *and* CORNWALL, *next* GONERIL, REGAN, CORDELIA,
with FOLLOWERS.*]*

Lear

Attend the Lords of France and Burgundy,
Gloucester.

Gloucester

I shall, my liege.

[Exeunt GLOUCESTER *and* EDMUND.*]*

Lear

35   Meantime we shall express our darker purpose.
Give me the map there. Know that we have
    divided
In three our kingdom; and 'tis our fast intent
To shake all cares and business from our age,
Conferring them on younger strengths, while we
Unburden'd crawl toward death. Our son of
40   Cornwall.
And you, our no less loving son of Albany.

We have this hour a constant will to publish
Our daughters' several dowers, that future strife
May be prevented now. The Princes, France and
    Burgundy,
Great rivals in our youngest daughter's love.   45
Long in our court have made their amorous
    sojourn.
And here are to be answer'd. Tell me, my
    daughters –
Since now we will divest us both of rule,
Interest of territory, cares of state –
Which of you shall we say doth love us most?   50
That we our largest bounty may extend
Where nature doth with merit challenge.
    Goneril,
Our eldest-born, speak first.

Goneril

Sir, I love you more than word can wield
    the matter;
Dearer than eyesight, space, and liberty;   55
Beyond what can be valued, rich or rare;
No less than life, with grace, health, beauty,
    honour;
As much as child e'er lov'd, or father found;
A love that makes breath poor and speech
    unable:
Beyond all manner of so much I love you.   60

Cordelia

[*Aside*] What shall Cordelia speak? Love, and be
    silent.

Lear

Of all these bounds, even from this line to
    this,
With shadowy forests and with champains
    rich'd,
With plenteous rivers and wide-skirted meads,
We make thee lady: to thine and Albany's
    issues
    65

Be this perpetual. – What says our second
daughter,
Our dearest Regan, wife of Cornwall? Speak.

Regan

I am made of that self metal as my sister,
And prize me at her worth. In my true heart
70   I find she names my very deed of love;
Only she comes too short, that I profess
Myself an enemy to all other joys
Which the most precious square of sense
possesses,
And find I am alone felicitate
In your dear Highness' love.

Cordelia

75   [Aside]   Then poor Cordelia!
And yet not so; since I am sure my love's
More ponderous than my tongue.

Lear

To thee and thine hereditary ever
Remain this ample third of our fair kingdom;
80   No less in space, validity, and pleasure,
Than that conferr'd on Goneril. – Now, our joy,
Although our last and least; to whose young
love
The vines of France and milk of Burgundy
Strive to be interess'd; what can you say to
draw
85   A third more opulent than your sisters? Speak.

Cordelia

Nothing, my lord.

Lear

Nothing!

Cordelia

Nothing.

Lear

Nothing will come of nothing. Speak again.

Cordelia

90   Unhappy that I am, I cannot heave

My heart into my mouth. I love your Majesty
According to my bond; no more nor less.
Lear
How, how, Cordelia! Mend your speech a little.
Lest you may mar your fortunes.
Cordelia
                                    Good my lord,
You have begot me, bred me, lov'd me; I   95
Return those duties back as are right fit,
Obey you, love you, and most honour you.
Why have my sisters husbands, if they say
They love you all? Haply, when I shall wed,
That lord whose hand must take my plight
        shall carry   100
Half my love with him, half my care and duty.
Sure I shall never marry like my sisters,
To love my father all.
Lear
But goes thy heart with this?
Cordelia
                                Ay, my good lord.
Lear
So young and so untender?   105
Cordelia
So young, my lord, and true.
Lear
Let it be so! Thy truth, then, be thy dower!
For, by the sacred radiance of the sun,
The mysteries of Hecat and the night;
By all the operation of the orbs   110
From whom we do exist and cease to be;
Here I disclaim all my paternal care,
Propinquity and property of blood,
And as a stranger to my heart and me
Hold thee from this for ever. The barbarous
        Scythian,   115
Or he that makes his generation messes
To gorge his appetite, shall to my bosom

Be as well neighbour'd, pitied, and reliev'd,
As thou my sometime daughter.

Kent

Good my liege –

Lear

120   Peace, Kent!
Come not between the dragon and his wrath.
I lov'd her most, and thought to set my rest
On her kind nursery. *[To CORDELIA]* Hence, and
    avoid my sight! –
So be my grave my peace as here I give
Her father's heart from her! Call France – Who
125   stirs?
Call Burgundy. Cornwall and Albany,
With my two daughters' dowers digest this
    third.
Let pride, which she calls plainness, marry
    her.
I do invest you jointly with my power,
130   Pre-eminence, and all the large effects
That troop with what majesty. Ourself, by
    monthly course,
With reservation of an hundred knights,
By you to be sustain'd, shall our abode
Make with you by due turn. Only we shall
    retain
135   The name, and all th' addition to a king:
The sway, revenue, execution of the rest,
Beloved sons, be yours; which to confirm,
This coronet part between you.

Kent

Royal Lear,
Whom I have ever honour'd as my king,
140   Lov'd as my father, as my master follow'd,
As my great patron thought on in my prayers –

Lear

The bow is bent and drawn; make from the
    shaft.

10

Kent
>   Let it fall rather, though the fork invade
>   The region of my heart. Be Kent unmannerly
>   When Lear is mad. What wouldst thou do, old
>   man?   145
>   Think'st thou that duty shall have dread to
>   speak
>   When power to flattery bows? To plainness
>   honour's bound
>   When majesty falls to folly. Reserve thy state;
>   And in thy best consideration check
>   This hideous rashness. Answer my life my
>   judgment: 150
>   Thy youngest daughter does not love thee
>   least;
>   Nor are those empty-hearted whose low sounds
>   Reverb no hollowness.

Lear
>   Kent, on thy life, no more!

Kent
>   My life I never held but as a pawn
>   To wage against thine enemies; nor fear to lose
>   it,   155
>   Thy safety being motive.

Lear
>   Out of my sight!

Kent
>   See better, Lear; and let me still remain
>   The true blank of thine eye.

Lear
>   Now by Apollo –

Kent
>   Now, by Apollo, King,
>   Thou swear'st thy gods in vain.

Lear
>   O, vassal! miscreant!   160

[Laying his hand on his sword.]

Albany and Cornwall
   Dear sir, forbear.
Kent
   Do;
   Kill thy physician, and the fee bestow
   Upon the foul disease. Revoke thy gift,
165   Or, whilst I can vent clamour from my throat,
   I'll tell thee thou dost evil.
Lear
                    Hear me, recreant;
   On thine allegiance, hear me.
   That thou hast sought to make us break our
      vows –
   Which we durst never yet – and with strain'd
      pride
170   To come betwixt our sentence and our power –
   Which nor our nature nor our place can bear;
   Our potency made good, take thy reward.
   Five days we do allot thee for provision
   To shield thee from disasters of the world.
175   And on the sixth to turn thy hated back
   Upon our kingdom; if, on the tenth day
      following,
   Thy banish'd trunk be found in our dominions,
   The moment is thy death. Away! by Jupiter.
   This shall not be revok'd.
Kent
180   Fare thee well. King. Sith thus thou wilt appear,
   Freedom lives hence, and banishment is here.
   [To CORDELIA] The gods to their dear shelter take
      thee, maid,
   That justly think'st, and hast most rightly said!
   [To REGAN and GONERIL] And your large speeches
      may your deeds approve,
185   That good effects may spring from words of love!
   Thus Kent, O princes, bids you all adieu;
   He'll shape his old course in a country new.

                    [Exit.]

[Flourish. Re-enter GLOUCESTER, *with* FRANCE,
BURGUNDY, *and* ATTENDANTS.]*

Gloucester

Here's France and Burgundy, my noble lord.

Lear

My Lord of Burgundy,
We first address toward you, who with this king 190
Hath rivall'd for our daughter. What in the
   least
Will you require in present dower with her,
Or cease your quest of love?

Burgundy

               Most royal Majesty,
I crave no more than hath your Highness offer'd,
Nor will you tender less.

Lear

              Right noble Burgundy, 195
When she was dear to us, we did hold her so;
But now her price is fallen. Sir, there she
   stands:
If aught within that little seeming substance,
Or all of it, with our displeasure piec'd,
And nothing more, may fitly like your Grace, 200
She's there, and she is yours.

Burgundy

             I know no answer.

Lear

Will you, with those infirmities she owes,
Unfriended, new-adopted to our hate,
Dower'd with our curse, and stranger'd with
   our oath,
Take her or leave her?

Burgundy

            Pardon me, royal sir; 205
Election makes not up in such conditions.

Lear

Then leave her, sir; for, by the pow'r that made
   me,

13

I tell you all her wealth. *[To* FRANCE*]* For you,
    great King,
I would not from your love make such a stray
To match you where I hate; therefore beseech
210   you
T'avert your liking a more worthier way,
Than on a wretch whom nature is asham'd
Almost t' acknowledge hers.

France

                    This is most strange.
That she, whom even but now was your best
    object,
The argument of your praise, balm of your
215   age,
The best, the dearest, should in this trice of
    time
Commit a thing so monstrous to dismantle
So many folds of favour. Sure her offence
Must be of such unnatural degree
220   That monsters it, or your fore-vouch'd affection
Fall into taint – which to believe of her
Must be a faith that reason without miracle
Should never plant in me.

Cordelia

                  I yet beseech your Majesty –
If for I want that glib and oily art
To speak and purpose not, since what I well
225   intend
I'll do't before I speak – that you make known
It is no vicious blot, murder, or foulness,
No unchaste action or dishonoured step,
That hath depriv'd me of your grace and
    favour;
230   But even for want of that for which I am richer –
A still-soliciting eye, and such a tongue
That I am glad I have not, though not to have
    it
Hath lost me in your liking.

Lear

                    Better thou
Hadst not been born than not t' have pleas'd
    me better.

France

    Is it but this? A tardiness in nature,   235
    Which often leaves the history unspoke
    That it intends to do! My Lord of Burgundy,
    What say you to the lady? Love's not love
    When it is mingled with regards that stands
    Aloof from th' entire point. Will you have her?   240
    She is herself a dowry.

Burgundy

                  Royal king,
    Give but that portion which yourself propos'd,
    And here I take Cordelia by the hand,
    Duchess of Burgundy.

Lear

    Nothing! I have sworn; I am firm.   245

Burgundy

    I am sorry, then, you have so lost a father
    That you must lose a husband.

Cordelia

                Peace be with Burgundy!
    Since that respects of fortune are his love
    I shall not be his wife.

France

    Fairest Cordelia, that art most rich, being
        poor;   250
    Most choice, forsaken; and most lov'd,
        despis'd!
    Thee and thy virtues here I seize upon,
    Be it lawful I take up what's cast away.
    Gods, gods! 'tis strange that from their cold'st
        neglect
    My love should kindle to inflam'd respect.   255
    Thy dow'rless daughter, King, thrown to my
        chance,

Is queen of us, of ours, and our fair France.
Not all the dukes of wat'rish Burgundy
Can buy this unpriz'd precious maid of me.
260 Bid them farewell, Cordelia, though unkind;
Thou losest here, a better where to find.

Lear
Thou hast her, France; let her be thine; for we
Have no such daughter, nor shall ever see
That face of hers again. *[To* CORDELIA*]* Therefore
be gone
265 Without our grace, our love, our benison.
Come, noble Burgundy.

[Flourish. Exeunt LEAR, BURGUNDY, CORNWALL, ALBANY,
GLOUCESTER, *and* ATTENDANTS.*]*

France
Bid farewell to your sisters.
Cordelia
The jewels of our father, with wash'd eyes
Cordelia leaves you. I know you what you are;
270 And, like a sister, am most loath to call
Your faults as they are named. Love well our
father.
To your professed bosoms I commit him;
But yet, alas, stood I within his grace,
I would prefer him to a better place.
275 So, farewell to you both.
Regan
Prescribe not us our duty.
Goneril
                                    Let your study
Be to content your lord, who hath receiv'd you
At fortune's alms. You have obedience scanted,
And well are worth the want that you have
wanted.
Cordelia
Time shall unfold what plighted cunning
280 hides,

16

Who covers faults, at last with shame derides.
Well may you prosper!

France

                        Come, my fair Cordelia.

[Exeunt FRANCE *and* CORDELIA.*]*

Goneril

Sister, it is not little I have to say of what most
nearly appertains to us both. I think our father
will hence to-night.   285

Regan

That's most certain, and with you; next month
with us.

Goneril

You see how full of changes his age is; the obser-
vation we have made of it hath not been little.
He always lov'd our sister most; and with what
poor judgment he hath now cast her off appears
too grossly.

Regan

'Tis the infirmity of his age; yet he hath ever but
slenderly known himself.   293

Goneril

The best and soundest of his time hath been but
rash; then must we look from his age to receive
not alone the imperfections of long-engraffed
condition, but therewithal the unruly waywardness that infirm and choleric years bring with
them.

Regan

Such unconstant starts are we like to have from
him as this of Kent's banishment.   300

Goneril

There is further compliment of leave-taking
between France and him. Pray you, let us hit
together; if our father carry authority with such
disposition as he bears, this last surrender of his
will but offend us.

Regan
305   We shall further think of it.

Goneril
We must do something, and i' th' heat.

[Exeunt.]

Scene II

Gloucester's castle.

[Enter EDMUND with a letter.]

Edmund — Struggles w/ being illegitimate
    Thou, Nature, art my goddess; to thy law
    My services are bound. Wherefore should I
    Stand in the plague of custom, and permit
    The curiosity of nations to deprive me,
    For that I am some twelve or fourteen
      moonshines   5
    Lag of a brother? Why bastard? Wherefore
      base?
    When my dimensions are as well compact,
    My mind as generous, and my shape as true,
    As honest madam's issue? Why brand they us
    With base? with baseness? bastardy? base, base?   10
    Who, in the lusty stealth of nature, take
    More composition and fierce quality
    Than doth, within a dull, stale, tired bed,
    Go to th' creating a whole tribe of fops
    Got 'tween asleep and wake? Well then,   15
    Legitimate Edgar, I must have your land.
    Our father's love is to the bastard Edmund
    As to th' legitimate. Fine word 'legitimate'!
    Well, my legitimate, if this letter speed,
    And my invention thrive, Edmund the base   20
    Shall top th' legitimate. I grow; I prosper.
    Now, gods, stand up for bastards.

[Enter GLOUCESTER.]

Gloucester
    Kent banish'd thus! and France in choler
      parted!
    And the King gone to-night! Prescrib'd his
      pow'r!
    Confin'd to exhibition! All this done   25

Upon the gad! Edmund, how now! What
news?

Edmund

So please your lordship, none.

[Putting up the letter.]

Gloucester

Why so earnestly seek you to put up that letter?

Edmund

I know no news, my lord.

Gloucester

30 What paper were you reading?

Edmund

Nothing, my lord.

Gloucester

No? What needed then that terrible dispatch of
it into your pocket? The quality of nothing hath
not such need to hide itself. Let's see. Come, if it
35 be nothing, I shall not need spectacles.

Edmund

I beseech you, sir, pardon me. It is a letter from
my brother that I have not all o'er-read; and for
so much as I have perus'd, I find it not fit for
your o'er-looking.

Gloucester

39 Give me the letter, sir.

Edmund

I shall offend either to detain or give it.
The contents, as in part I understand them, are
to blame.

Gloucester

Let's see, let's see.

Edmund

I hope, for my brother's justification, he wrote
44 this but as an essay or taste of my virtue.

Gloucester

[Reads] 'This policy and reverence of age makes
the world bitter to the best of our times; keeps

our fortunes from us till our oldness cannot relish them. I begin to find an idle and fond bondage in the oppression of aged tyranny, who sways, not as it hath power, but as it is suffer'd. Come to me, that of this I may speak more. If our father would sleep till I wak'd him, you should enjoy half his revenue for ever, and live the beloved of your brother. EDGAR.' Hum – Conspiracy! 'Sleep till I wak'd him, you should enjoy half his revenue.' My son Edgar! Had he a hand to write this? a heart and a brain to breed it in? When came this to you? Who brought it?

51

Edmund

It was not brought to me, my lord; there's the cunning of it. I found it thrown in at the casement of my closet.

58

Gloucester

You know the character to be your brother's?

Edmund

If the matter were good, my lord, I durst swear it were his; but in respect of that, I would fain think it were not.

62

Gloucester

It is his.

Edmund

It is his hand, my lord; but I hope his heart is not in the contents.

65

Gloucester

Has he never before sounded you in this
business?

Edmund

Never, my lord; but I have heard him oft maintain it to be fit that, sons at perfect age and fathers declin'd, the father should be as ward to the son, and the son manage his revenue.

71

Gloucester

O villain, villain! His very opinion in the letter! Abhorred villain! Unnatural, detested, brutish

villain! Worse than brutish! Go, sirrah, seek him;
I'll apprehend him. Abominable villain! Where is
75 he?

Edmund

I do not well know, my lord. If it shall please you
to suspend your indignation against my brother
till you can derive from him better testimony of
his intent, you should run a certain course; where,
if you violently proceed against him, mistaking
his purpose, it would make a great gap in your
own honour, and shake in pieces the heart of his
obedience. I dare pawn down my life for him that
he hath writ this to feel my affection to your
honour, and to no other pretence of danger.

Gloucester

85 Think you so?

Edmund

If your honour judge it meet, I will place you
where you shall hear us confer of this, and by an
auricular assurance have your satisfaction; and
that without any further delay than this very
evening.

Gloucester

90 He cannot be such a monster.

Edmund

Nor is not, sure.

Gloucester

To his father, that so tenderly and entirely loves
him. Heaven and earth! Edmund, seek him out;
wind me into him, I pray you. Frame the business
after your own wisdom. I would unstate myself
96 to be in a due resolution.

Edmund

I will seek him, sir, presently; convey the business
as I shall find means, and acquaint you withal.

Gloucester

These late eclipses in the sun and moon portend
no good to us. Though the wisdom of nature can

22

reason it thus and thus, yet nature finds itself scourg'd by the sequent effects: love cools, friendship falls off, brothers divide; in cities, mutinies; in countries, discord; in palaces, treason; and the bond crack'd 'twixt son and father. This villain of mine comes under the prediction: there's son against father. The King falls from bias of nature: there's father against child. We have seen the best of our time: machinations, hollowness, treachery, and all ruinous disorders, follow us disquietly to our graves. Find out this villain, Edmund; it shall lose thee nothing; do it carefully. And the noble and true-hearted Kent banish'd! His offence, honesty! 'Tis strange.

[Exit.]

Edmund

This is the excellent foppery of the world, that, when we are sick in fortune, often the surfeits of our own behaviour, we make guilty of our disasters the sun, the moon, and stars; as if we were villains on necessity; fools by heavenly compulsion; knaves, thieves, and treachers, by spherical predominance; drunkards, liars, and adulterers, by an enforc'd obedience of planetary influence; and all that we are evil in, by a divine thrusting on – an admirable evasion of whoremaster man, to lay his goatish disposition on the charge of a star! My father compounded with my mother under the Dragon's tail, and my nativity was under Ursa Major, so that it follows I am rough and lecherous. Fut, I should have been that I am, had the maidenliest star in the firmament twinkled on my bastardizing. Edgar!

[Enter EDGAR.]

Pat! He comes like the catastrophe of the old comedy. My cue is villainous melancholy, with a

127

sigh like Tom o' Bedlam. – O, these eclipses do
131   portend these divisions! fa, sol, la, mi.

Edgar

How now, brother Edmund! What serious
contemplation are you in?

Edmund

I am thinking, brother, of a prediction I read this
135   other day what should follow these eclipses.

Edgar

Do you busy yourself with that?

Edmund

I promise you, the effects he writes of succeed
unhappily; as of unnaturalness between the
child and the parent; death, dearth, dissolutions
of ancient amities; divisions in state, menaces
and maledictions against king and nobles; need-
less diffidences, banishment of friends, dissipation
of cohorts, nuptial breaches, and I know not
142   what.

Edgar

How long have you been a sectary astronomical?

Edmund

Come, come! When saw you my father last?

Edgar

145   The night gone by.

Edmund

Spake you with him?

Edgar

Ay, two hours together.

Edmund

Parted you in good terms? Found you no
displeasure in him by word nor countenance?

Edgar

150   None at all.

Edmund

Bethink yourself wherein you may have offended
him; and at my entreaty forbear his presence,
until some little time hath qualified the heat of

his displeasure, which at this instant so rageth
in him that with the mischief of your person it
would scarcely allay.   155

Edgar

Some villain hath done me wrong.

Edmund

That's my fear. I pray you have a continent
forbearance till the speed of his rage goes slower;
and, as I say, retire with me to my lodging, from
whence I will fitly bring you to hear my lord
speak. Pray ye go; there's my key. If you do stir
abroad, go arm'd.   161

Edgar

Arm'd, brother!

Edmund

Brother, I advise you to the best. I am no honest
man if there be any good meaning toward you.
I have told you what I have seen and heard – but
faintly; nothing like the image and horror of it.
Pray you, away.   167

Edgar

Shall I hear from you anon?

Edmund

I do serve you in this business.

[Exit EDGAR.]

A credulous father! and a brother noble,
Whose nature is so far from doing harms
That he suspects none; on whose foolish
    honesty
My practices ride easy! I see the business.
Let me, if not by birth, have lands by wit:
All with me's meet that I can fashion fit.   175

[Exit.]

Scene III

The Duke of Albany's palace

[Enter GONERIL *and* OSWALD, *her steward.]*

Goneril
Did my father strike my gentleman for chiding
of his fool?

Oswald
Ay, madam.

Goneril
By day and night, he wrongs me; every hour
5   He flashes into one gross crime or other
That sets us all at odds. I'll not endure it.
His knights grow riotous, and himself upbraids
us
On every trifle. When he returns from hunting,
I will not speak with him; say I am sick.
10   If you come slack of former services,
You shall do well; the fault of it I'll answer.

[Horns within.]

Oswald
He's coming, madam; I hear him.

Goneril
Put on what weary negligence you please,
You and your fellows; I'd have it come to
question.
15   If he distaste it, let him to my sister,
Whose mind and mine, I know, in that are
one,
Not to be overrul'd. Idle old man,
That still would manage those authorities
That he hath given away! Now, by my life,
20   Old fools are babes again, and must be us'd
With checks as flatteries, when they are seen
abus'd.
Remember what I have said.

Oswald

Well, madam.

Goneril

And let his knights have colder looks among
you;
What grows of it, no matter. Advise your
fellows so.
I would breed from hence occasions, and I
shall,
That I may speak. I'll write straight to my sister
To hold my very course. Prepare for dinner.

25

[Exeunt.]

Scene IV

A hall in Albany's palace.

[Enter KENT, *disguised.]*

Kent
> If but as well I other accents borrow
> That can my speech defuse, my good intent
> May carry through itself to that full issue
> For which I raz'd my likeness. Now, banish'd Kent,
> If thou canst serve where thou dost stand
>   condemn'd,
5
> So may it come thy master whom thou lov'st
> Shall find thee full of labours.

[Horns within. Enter LEAR, KNIGHTS, *and* ATTENDANTS.*]*

Lear
> Let me not stay a jot for dinner; go get it ready.
> *[Exit an Attendant]* How now! What art thou?

Kent
10
> A man, sir.

Lear
> What dost thou profess? What wouldst thou
>   with us?

Kent
> I do profess to be no less than I seem, to serve
> him truly that will put me in trust, to love him
> that is honest, to converse with him that is wise
> and says little, to fear judgment, to fight when I
17
> cannot choose, and to eat no fish.

Lear
> What art thou?

Kent
> A very honest-hearted fellow, and as poor as the
20
> King.

Lear
> If thou be'st as poor for a subject as he's for a
> king, thou art poor enough. What wouldst thou?

Kent
Service.

Lear
Who wouldst thou serve?

Kent
You.   25

Lear
Dost thou know me, fellow?

Kent
No, sir; but you have that in your countenance
which I would fain call master.

Lear
What's that?

Kent
Authority.   30

Lear
What services canst thou do?

Kent
I can keep honest counsel, ride, run, mar a curious
tale in telling it, and deliver a plain message
bluntly. That which ordinary men are fit for, I am
qualified in; and the best of me is diligence.   35

Lear
How old art thou?

Kent
Not so young, sir, to love a woman for singing,
nor so old to dote on her for anything: I have
years on my back forty-eight.   39

Lear
Follow me; thou shalt serve me. If I like thee no
worse after dinner, I will not part from thee yet.
Dinner, ho, dinner! Where's my knave? my fool?
– Go you and call my fool hither.

[Exit an ATTENDANT.*]*

[Enter OSWALD.*]*

You, you, sirrah, where's my daughter?   44

29

Oswald
So please you –

[Exit.]

Lear
What says the fellow there? Call the clotpoll back.
[Exit a Knight] Where's my fool, ho? I think the
world's asleep.

[Re-enter KNIGHT.*]*

How now! Where's that mongrel?
Knight
50   He says, my lord, your daughter is not well.
Lear
Why came not the slave back to me when I call'd
him?
Knight
Sir, he answered me in the roundest manner he
would not.
Lear
55   He would not!
Knight
My lord, I know not what the matter is; but, to
my judgment, your Highness is not entertain'd
with that ceremonious affection as you were wont;
there's a great abatement of kindness appears as
well in the general dependants as in the Duke
61   himself also and your daughter.
Lear
Ha! say'st thou so?
Knight
I beseech you pardon me, my lord, if I be
mistaken; for my duty cannot be silent when I
65   think your Highness wrong'd.
Lear
Thou but rememb'rest me of mine own concep-
tion. I have perceived a most faint neglect of late,
which I have rather blamed as mine own jealous

curiosity than as a very pretence and purpose of
unkindness. I will look further into't. But where's
my fool? I have not seen him this two days.   71

Knight

Since my young lady's going into France, sir, the
fool hath much pined away.

Lear

No more of that; I have noted it well. Go you
and tell my daughter I would speak with her.
[Exit an Attendant] Go you, call hither my fool.

[Exit another ATTENDANT.]

[Re-enter OSWALD.]

O, you sir, you! Come you hither, sir.
Who am I, sir?   77

Oswald

My lady's father.

Lear

'My lady's father'! my lord's knave! you whoreson
dog! you slave! you cur!   80

Oswald

I am none of these, my lord; I beseech your
pardon.

Lear

Do you bandy looks with me, you rascal!
[Striking him.]

Oswald

I'll not be strucken, my lord.   84

Kent

Nor tripp'd neither, you base foot-ball player.
[Tripping up his heels.]

Lear

I thank thee, fellow; thou serv'st me, and I'll love
thee.   87

Kent

Come, sir, arise, away! I'll teach you differences.
Away, away! If you will measure your lubber's

length again, tarry; but away! Go to! Have you
wisdom? So.

[Pushes OSWALD *out.]*

Lear

Now, my friendly knave, I thank thee: there's
93   earnest of thy service.

[Giving KENT *money.]*

[Enter FOOL.*]*

Fool

Let me hire him too; here's my coxcomb.

[Offering KENT *his cap.]*

Lear

95   How now, my pretty knave! How dost thou?
Fool

Sirrah, you were best take my coxcomb.
Kent

Why, fool?
Fool

Why? For taking one's part that's out of favour.
Nay, an thou canst not smile as the wind sits,
thou 'It catch cold shortly. There, take my
coxcomb. Why, this fellow has banish'd two on's
daughters, and did the third a blessing against
his will; if thou follow him, thou must needs wear
my coxcomb. – How now, nuncle! Would I had
two coxcombs and two daughters!

Lear

105   Why, my boy?
Fool

If I gave them all my living, I'd keep my coxcombs
myself. There's mine; beg another of thy
daughters.

Lear

109   Take heed, sirrah – the whip.

Fool
> Truth's a dog must to kennel; he must be whipp'd
> out, when Lady the brach may stand by th'fire
> and stink.

Lear
> A pestilent gall to me!

Fool
> Sirrah, I'll teach thee a speech.

Lear
> Do.   115

Fool
> Mark it, nuncle:
> Have more than thou showest,
> Speak less than thou knowest,
> Lend less than thou owest,
> Ride more than thou goest,   120
> Learn more than thou trowest,
> Set less than thou throwest;
> Leave thy drink and thy whore,
> And keep in-a-door,
> And thou shalt have more   125
> Than two tens to a score.

Kent
> This is nothing, fool.

Fool
> Then 'tis like the breath of an un-fee'd lawyer –
> you gave me nothing for't. Can you make no use
> of nothing, nuncle?   130

Lear
> Why, no, boy; nothing can be made out of nothing.

Fool
> *[To KENT]* Prithee tell him, so much the rent of
> his land comes to; he will not believe a fool.

Lear
> A bitter fool!

Fool
> Dost thou know the difference, my boy, between   135
> a biter bitter fool and a sweet one?

33

Lear

    No, lad; teach me.

Fool

    That lord that counsell'd thee

140
        To give away thy land,
        Come place him here by me –
        Do thou for him stand.
    The sweet and bitter fool
        Will presently appear;
145
    The one in motley here,
        The other found out there.

Lear

    Dost thou call me fool, boy?

Fool

    All thy other titles thou hast given away; that
149   thou wast born with.

Kent

    This is not altogether fool, my lord.

Fool

    No, faith, lords and great men will not let me; if
    I had a monopoly out, they would have part on't.
    And ladies too – they will not let me have all the
    fool to myself; they'll be snatching. Nuncle, give
155   me an egg, and I'll give thee two crowns.

Lear

    What two crowns shall they be?

Fool

    Why, after I have cut the egg i' th' middle and
    eat up the meat, the two crowns of the egg. When
    thou clovest thy crown i' th' middle, and gav'st
    away both parts, thou bor'st thine ass on thy back
    o'er the dirt. Thou hadst little wit in thy bald
    crown when thou gav'st thy golden one away. If
    I speak like myself in this, let him be whipp'd
163   that first finds it so.

    [Sings] Fools had ne'er less grace in a year;
        For wise men are grown foppish,

And know not how their wits to wear,
Their manners are so apish.

Lear

When were you wont to be so full of songs,
sirrah? 169

Fool

I have us'd it, nuncle, e'er since thou mad'st thy
daughters thy mothers; for when thou gav'st them
the rod, and put'st down thine own breeches
[Sings] Then they for sudden joy did weep,
        And I for sorrow sung,
            That such a king should play bo-peep 175
            And go the fools among.
Prithee, nuncle, keep a schoolmaster that can
teach thy fool to lie. I would fain learn to lie.

Lear

An you lie, sirrah, we'll have you whipp'd. 179

Fool

I marvel what kin thou and thy daughters are.
They'll have me whipp'd for speaking true: thou'lt
have me whipp'd for lying; and sometimes I am
whipp'd for holding my peace. I had rather be
any kind o' thing than a fool; and yet I would
not be thee, nuncle; thou hast pared thy wit o'
both sides, and left nothing i' th' middle. Here
comes one o' th' parings. 186

[Enter GONERIL.*]*

Lear

How now, daughter! What makes that frontlet
on? You are too much of late i' th' frown. 188

Fool

Thou wast a pretty fellow when thou hadst no
need to care for her frowning; now thou art an
O without a figure. I am better than thou art now:
I am a fool, thou art nothing. *[To* GONERIL*]* Yes,
forsooth, I will hold my tongue; so your face bids
me, though you say nothing. Mum, mum!

He that keeps nor crust nor crumb.
197   Weary of all, shall want some.
   [Pointing to Lear] That's a sheal'd peascod.

Goneril

  Not only, sir, this your all-licens'd fool,
200 But other of your insolent retinue
  Do hourly carp and quarrel, breaking forth
  In rank and not-to-be-endured riots. Sir,
  I had thought, by making this well known unto
   you,
  To have found a safe redress; but now grow
   fearful,
205 By what yourself too late have spoke and done,
  That you protect this course, and put it on
  By your allowance; which if you should, the fault
  Would not scape censure, nor the redresses
   sleep,
  Which, in the tender of a wholesome weal,
210 Might in their working do you that offence
  Which else were shame, that then necessity
  Will call discreet proceeding.

Fool

  For, you know, nuncle,
  The hedge-sparrow fed the cuckoo so long
215 That it had it head bit off by it young.
  So, out went the candle, and we were left
   darkling.

Lear

  Are you our daughter?

Goneril

  I would you would make use of your good
   wisdom,
220 Whereof I know you are fraught, and put away
  These dispositions which of late transport you
  From what you rightly are.

Fool

  May not an ass know when the cart draws the
   horse? Whoop, Jug! I love thee.

Lear

Does any here know me? This is not Lear.   225
Does Lear walk thus? speak thus? Where are his
      eyes?
Either his notion weakens, or his discernings
Are lethargied. – Ha! waking? 'Tis not so. –
Who is it that can tell me who I am?

Fool

Lear's shadow.   230

Lear

I would learn that; for, by the marks of sovereignty, knowledge, and reason, I should be false
persuaded I had daughters,

Fool

Which they will make an obedient father.

Lear

Your name, fair gentlewoman?   235

Goneril

This admiration, sir, is much o' th' savour
Of other your new pranks. I do beseech you
To understand my purposes aright.
As you are old and reverend, should be wise.
Here do you keep a hundred knights and squires;   240
Men so disorder'd, so debosh'd and bold,
That this our court, infected with their
      manners.
Shows like a riotous inn. Epicurism and lust
Makes it more like a tavern or a brothel
Than a grac'd palace. The shame itself doth speak 245
For instant remedy. Be then desir'd
By her that else will take the thing she begs
A little to disquantity your train;
And the remainders that shall still depend
To be such men as may besort your age,   250
Which know themselves and you.

Lear

                              Darkness and devils!
Saddle my horses; call my train together.

Degenerate bastard! I'll not trouble thee;
Yet have I left a daughter.

Goneril,
You strike my people; and your disorder'd
255   rabble
Make servants of their betters.

[Enter ALBANY.]

Lear
Woe that too late repents! – O, sir, are you come?
Is it your will? Speak, sir. – Prepare my horses.
Ingratitude, thou marble-hearted fiend,
260   More hideous when thou show'st thee in a child
Than the sea-monster!

Albany
                    Pray, sir, be patient.

Lear
[To GONERIL] Detested kite! thou liest:
My train are men of choice and rarest parts,
That all particulars of duty know;
265   And in the most exact regard support
The worships of their name. – O most small
    fault,
How ugly didst thou in Cordelia show!
Which, like an engine, wrench'd my frame of
    nature
From the fix'd place; drew from my heart all
    love
270   And added to the gall. O Lear, Lear, Lear!
Beat at this gate that let thy folly in

[Striking his head.]

And thy dear judgment out! Go, go, my people.

[Exeunt KENT and KNIGHTS.]

Albany
My lord, I am guiltless, as I am ignorant
Of what hath moved you.

Lear

                    It may be so, my lord.
Hear, Nature, hear; dear goddess, hear.   275
Suspend thy purpose, if thou didst intend
To make this creature fruitful.
Into her womb convey sterility;
Dry up in her the organs of increase;
And from her derogate body never spring   280
A babe to honour her! If she must teem,
Create her child of spleen, that it may live
And be a thwart disnatur'd torment to her.
Let it stamp wrinkles in her brow of youth,
With cadent tears fret channels in her cheeks,   285
Turn all her mother's pains and benefits
To laughter and contempt, that she may feel
How sharper than a serpent's tooth it is
To have a thankless child. Away, away!

           [Exit.]

Albany

Now, gods that we adore, where of comes
    this?   290

Goneril

Never afflict yourself to know more of it;
But let his disposition have that scope
As dotage gives it.

           [Re-enter LEAR.*]*

Lear

What, fifty of my followers at a clap!
Within a fortnight!

Albany

           What's the matter, sir?   295

Lear

I'll tell thee. *[To* GONERIL*]* Life and death! I am
    asham'd
That thou hast power to shake my manhood
    thus;

That these hot tears, which break from me
    perforce,
Should make thee worth them. Blasts and fogs
    upon thee!
300 Th' untented woundings of a father's curse
Pierce every sense about thee! – Old fond eyes,
Beweep this cause again, I'll pluck ye out,
And cast you, with the waters that you loose,
To temper clay. Ha! Is't come to this?
305 Let it be so. I have another daughter,
Who, I am sure, is kind and comfortable.
When she shall hear this of thee, with her nails
She'll flay thy wolfish visage. Thou shalt find
That I'll resume the shape which thou dost
    think
310 I have cast off for ever.

[Exit LEAR.*]*

Goneril
                Do you mark that?
Albany
I cannot be so partial, Goneril,
To the great love I bear you –
Goneril
Pray you, content. – What, Oswald, ho!
[To the FOOL*]* You, sir, more knave than fool,
315   after your master.
Fool
Nuncle Lear, nuncle Lear, tarry – take the fool
with thee.
        A fox, when one has caught her,
        And such a daughter,
320   Should sure to the slaughter,
        If my cap would buy a halter.
        So the fool follows after.

[Exit.]

Goneril

This man hath had good counsel. A hundred
knights!
'Tis politic and safe to let him keep
At point a hundred knights – yes, that on every
dream,   325
Each buzz, each fancy, each complaint, dislike,
He may enguard his dotage with their pow'rs,
And hold our lives in mercy. Oswald, I say!

Albany

Well, you may fear too far.

Goneril

                              Safer than trust too far.
Let me still take away the harms I fear,   330
Not fear still to be taken. I know his heart.
What he hath utter'd I have writ my sister.
If she sustain him and his hundred knights,
When I have show'd th' unfitness –

[Re-enter OSWALD.]

                              How now, Oswald!
What, have you writ that letter to my sister?   335

Oswald

Ay, madam.

Goneril

Take you some company, and away to horse;
Inform her full of my particular fear,
And thereto add such reasons of your own
As may compact it more. Get you gone;   340
And hasten your return. *[Exit OSWALD]* No, no,
my lord,
This milky gentleness and course of yours,
Though I condemn not, yet, under pardon,
You are much more ataxt for want of wisdom
Than prais'd for harmful mildness.   345

Albany

How far your eyes may pierce I cannot tell.
Striving to better, oft we mar what's well.

41

Goneril
   Nay, then –
Albany
   Well, well; th' event.

[Exeunt.]

Scene V

Court before the Duke of Albany's palace.

[Enter LEAR, KENT, and FOOL.]

Lear

Go you before to Gloucester with these letters.
Acquaint my daughter no further with anything
you know than comes from her demand out of
the letter. If your diligence be not speedy, I shall
be there afore you.   4

Kent

I will not sleep, my lord, till I have delivered your
letter.

[Exit]

Fool

If a man's brains were in's heels, were't not in
danger of kibes?

Lear

Ay, boy.

Fool

Then, I prithee, be merry; thy wit shall not go
slipshod.   11

Lear

Ha, ha, ha!

Fool

Shalt see thy other daughter will use thee kindly;
for though she's as like this as a crab's like an
apple, yet I can tell what I can tell.   15

Lear

What canst tell, boy?

Fool

She will taste as like this as a crab does to a crab.
Thou canst tell why one's nose stands i' th' middle
on's face?

Lear

No.   20

Fool

Why to keep one's eyes of either side's nose, that
what a man cannot smell out, he may spy into.

Lear

I did her wrong.

Fool

Canst tell how an oyster makes his shell?

Lear

25 No.

Fool

Nor I neither; but I can tell why a snail has a
house.

Lear

Why?

Fool

Why, to put's head in; not to give it away to his
30 daughters, and leave his horns without a case.

Lear

I will forget my nature. So kind a father! –
Be my horses ready?

Fool

Thy asses are gone about 'em. The reason why
the seven stars are no more than seven is a pretty
reason.

Lear

35 Because they are not eight?

Fool

Yes, indeed. Thou wouldst make a good fool.

Lear

To take't again perforce! Monster ingratitude!

Fool

If thou wert my fool, nuncle, I'd have thee beaten
for being old before thy time.

Lear

40 How's that?

Fool

Thou shouldst not have been old till thou hadst
been wise.

Lear

O, let me not be mad, not mad, sweet heaven!
Keep me in temper; I would not be mad!

[Enter GENTLEMAN.]

How now! are the horses ready?   45

Gentleman

Ready, my lord.

Lear

Come, boy.

Fool

She that's a maid now, and laughs at my
        departure,
Shall not be a maid long, unless things be cut
        shorter.

[Exeunt.]

ACT TWO
Scene I

A court-yard in the Earl of Gloucester's castle.

[*Enter* EDMUND *and* CURAN, *meeting.*]

Edmund
    Save thee, Curan.
Curan
    And you, sir. I have been with your father, and
    given him notice that the Duke of Cornwall and
    Regan his Duchess will be here with him this night.
Edmund
5   How comes that?
Curan
    Nay. I know not. You have heard of the news
    abroad; I mean the whisper'd one, for they are
    yet but ear-bussing arguments?
Edmund
    Not I. Pray you, what are they?
Curan
    Have you heard of no likely wars toward 'twixt
11   the Dukes of Cornwall and Albany?
Edmund
    Not a word.
Curan
    You may do, then, in time. Fare you well, sir.

[*Exit.*]

Edmund
    The Duke be here to-night? The better! best!
15   This weaves itself perforce into my business.
    My father hath set guard to take my brother;
    And I have one thing, of a queasy question,
    Which I must act. Briefness and fortune work!
    Brother, a word! Descend. Brother, I say!

[Enter EDGAR.]

My father watches. O sir, fly this place;   20
Intelligence is given where you are hid;
You have now the good advantage of the night.
Have you not spoken 'gainst the Duke of
    Cornwall?
He's coming hither, now, i' th' night, i' th'
    haste,
And Regan with him. Have you nothing said   25
Upon his party 'gainst the Duke of Albany?
Advise yourself.

Edgar

            I am sure on't, not a word.

Edmund

I hear my father coming. Pardon me,
In cunning I must draw my sword upon you.
Draw; seem to defend yourself; now quit you
    well. –
Yield; come before my father. Light, ho, here! –   30
Fly, brother. – Torches, torches! – So, farewell.

[Exit EDGAR.]

Some blood drawn on me would beget opinion

[Wounds his arm.]

Of my more fierce endeavour. I have seen
    drunkards
Do more than this in sport. – Father, father!   35
Stop, stop! No help?

[Enter GLOUCESTER, and SERVANTS with torches.]

Gloucester

Now, Edmund, where's the villain?

Edmund

Here stood he in the dark, his sharp sword out,
Mumbling of wicked charms, conjuring the
    moon
To stand's auspicious mistress.

Gloucester

40   But where is he?

Edmund
  Look, sir, I bleed.

Gloucester

                          Where is the villain, Edmund?

Edmund
  Fled this way, sir. When by no means he could –

Gloucester
  Pursue him, ho! Go after. *[Exeunt* SERVANTS*]* – By
  no means what?

Edmund
  Persuade me to the murder of your lordship;
45 But that I told him the revenging gods
  'Gainst parricides did all their thunders bend;
  Spoke with how manifold and strong a bond
  The child was bound to th' father. Sir, in fine,
  Seeing how loathly opposite I stood
50 To his unnatural purpose, in fell motion,
  With his prepared sword, he charges home
  My unprovided body, latch'd mine arm;
  But when he saw my best alarum'd spirits,
  Bold in the quarrel's right, rous'd to th'
      encounter,
55 Or whether gasted by the noise I made,
  Full suddenly he fled.

Gloucester

                          Let him fly far.
  Not in this land shall he remain uncaught;
  And found – dispatch. The noble Duke my
      master,
  My worthy arch and patron, comes to-night;
60 By his authority I will proclaim it,
  That he which finds him shall deserve our
      thanks,
  Bringing the murderous coward to the stake;
  He that conceals him, death.

Edmund

When I dissuaded him from his intent,
And found him pight to do it, with curst
speech   65
I threaten'd to discover him; he replied,
'Thou unpossessing bastard! dost thou think,
If I would stand against thee, would the
reposure
Of any trust, virtue, or worth, in thee
Make thy words faith'd? No. What I should
deny –   70
As this I would; ay, though thou didst produce
My very character – I'd turn it all
To thy suggestion, plot, and damned practice;
And thou must make a dullard of the world,
If they not thought the profits of my death   75
Were very pregnant and potential spurs
To make thee seek it'.

Gloucester

        O strong and fast'ned villain!
Would he deny his letter? – I never got him.

[Tucket within.]

Hark, the Duke's trumpets! I know not why he
comes.
All ports I'll bar; the villain shall not scape;   80
The Duke must grant me that. Besides, his
picture
I will send far and near, that all the kingdom
May have due note of him; and of my land,
Loyal and natural boy, I'll work the means
To make thee capable.   85

[Enter CORNWALL, REGAN, *and* ATTENDANTS.*]*

Cornwall

How now, my noble friend! since I came hither,
Which I can call but now, I have heard strange
news.

Regan
>   If it be true, all vengeance comes too short
>   Which can pursue th' offender. How dost, my
>   lord?

Gloucester
90   O, madam, my old heart is crack'd, it's crack'd!

Regan
>   What, did my father's godson seek your life?
>   He whom my father nam'd? your Edgar?

Gloucester
>   O lady, lady, shame would have it hid!

Regan
>   Was he not companion with the riotous
>   knights
95   That tend upon my father?

Gloucester
>   I know not, madam. 'Tis too bad, too bad.

Edmund
>   Yes, madam, he was of that consort.

Regan
>   No marvel, then, though he were ill affected.
>   'Tis they have put him on the old man's death,
100 To have th' expense and waste of his revenues.
>   I have this present evening from my sister
>   Been well inform'd of them; and with such
>   cautions
>   That, if they come to sojourn at my house,
>   I'll not be there.

Cornwall
>   Nor I, assure thee, Regan.
>   Edmund, I hear that you have shown your
105   father
>   A child-like office.

Edmund
>   It was my duty, sir.

Gloucester
>   He did bewray his practice, and receiv'd
>   This hurt you see, striving to apprehend him.

Cornwall
  Is he pursued?
Gloucester

              Ay, my good lord.
Cornwall
  If he be taken, he shall never more   110
  Be fear'd of doing harm. Make your own
    purpose,
  How in my strength you please. For you,
    Edmund,
  Whose virtue and obedience doth this instant
  So much commend itself, you shall be ours.
  Natures of such deep trust we shall much need; 115
  You we first seize on.
Edmund

             I shall serve you, sir,
  Truly, however else.
Gloucester

          For him I thank your Grace.
Cornwall
  You know not why we came to visit you –
Regan
  Thus out of season, threading dark-ey'd night:
  Occasions, noble Gloucester, of some poise,   120
  Wherein we must have use of your advice.
  Our father he hath writ, so hath our sister,
  Of differences, which I best thought it fit
  To answer from our home; the several
    messengers
  From hence attend dispatch. Our good old
    friend,   125
  Lay comforts to your bosom, and bestow
  Your needful counsel to our businesses,
  Which craves the instant use.
Gloucester

              I serve you, madam.
  Your Graces are right welcome.

[Exeunt.]

Scene II.

Before Gloucester's castle.

[Enter KENT and OSWALD severally.]

Oswald
Good dawning to thee, friend Art of this house?

Kent
Ay.

Oswald
Where may we set our horses?

Kent
I' th' mire.

Oswald
Prithee, if thou lov'st me, tell me.

5 **Kent**
I love thee not.

Oswald
Why then, I care not for thee.

Kent
If I had thee in Lipsbury pinfold, I would make
thee care for me.

Oswald
10 Why dost thou use me thus? I know thee not.

Kent
Fellow, I know thee.

Oswald
What dost thou know me for?

Kent
A knave, a rascal, an eater of broken meats; a base,
proud, shallow, beggarly, three-suited, hundred-
pound, filthy, worsted-stocking knave; a lily-liver'd,
action-taking, whoreson, glass-gazing, super-
serviceable, finical rogue; one-trunk-inheriting
slave; one that wouldst be a bawd in way of good
service, and art nothing but the composition of
a knave, beggar, coward, pander, and the son and
heir of a mongrel bitch; one whom I will beat

into clamorous whining, if thou deny'st the least
syllable of thy addition.

Oswald

Why, what a monstrous fellow art thou, thus to
rail on one that is neither known of thee nor
knows thee?   24

Kent

What a brazen-face'd varlet art thou, to deny
thou knowest me! Is it two days since I tripp'd
up thy heels and beat thee before the King? Draw,
you rogue; for, though it be night, yet the moon
shines; I'll make a sop o' th moonshine of you;
you whoreson cullionly barber-monger, draw.

[Drawing his sword.]

Oswald

Away! I have nothing to do with thee.   31

Kent

Draw, you rascal. You come with letters against
the King, and take Vanity the puppet's part against
the royalty of her father. Draw, you rogue, or I'll
so carbonado your shanks. Draw, you rascal; come
your ways.

Oswald

Help, ho! murder! help.   36

Kent

Strike, you slave; stand, rogue, stand; you neat
slave, strike. *[Beating him.]*

Oswald

Help, ho! murder! murder!

[Enter EDMUND *with his rapier drawn,* GLOUCESTER,
CORNWALL, REGAN *and* SERVANTS,*]*

Edmund

How now! What's the matter? Part!   40

Kent

With you, godman boy, an you please.
Come, I'll flesh ye; come on, young master.

Gloucester
 Weapons! arms! What's the matter here?
Cornwall
 Keep peace, upon your lives;
45 He dies that strikes again. What is the matter?
Regan
 The messengers from our sister and the King.
Cornwall
 What is your difference? Speak.
Oswald
 I am scarce in breath, my lord.
Kent
 No marvel, you have so bestirr'd your valour. You
 cowardly rascal, nature disclaims in thee: a tailor
51 made thee.
Cornwall
 Thou art a strange fellow. A tailor make a man?
Kent
 Ay, a tailor, sir. A stone-cutter or a painter could
 not have made him so ill, though they had been
55 but two years o' th' trade.
Cornwall
 Speak yet, how grew your quarrel?
Oswald
 This ancient ruffian, sir, whose life I have spar'd
 at suit of his grey beard –
Kent
 Thou whoreson zed! thou unnecessary letter! My
 lord, if you will give me leave, I will tread this
 unbolted villain into mortar, and daub the wall of
62 a jakes with him. – Spare my grey beard, you wagtail?
Cornwall
 Peace, sirrah!
 You beastly knave, know you no reverence?
Kent
65 Yes, sir; but anger hath a privilege.
Cornwall
 Why art thou angry?

Kent

That such a slave as this should wear a sword,
Who wears no honesty. Such smiling rogues as
    these,
Like rats, oft bite the holy cords a-twain
Which are too intrinse t' unloose; smooth every
    passion   70
That in the natures of their lords rebel;
Bring oil to fire, snow to their colder moods;
Renege, affirm, and turn their halcyon beaks
With every gale and vary of their masters,
Knowing nought, like dogs, but following.   75
A plague upon your epileptic visage!
Smile you my speeches, as I were a fool?
Goose, if I had you upon Sarum plain,
I'd drive ye cackling home to Camelot.

Cornwall

What, are thou mad, old fellow?   80

Gloucester

How fell you out? Say that.

Kent

No contraries hold more antipathy
Than I and such a knave.

Cornwall

Why dost thou call him knave? What is his fault?

Kent

His countenance likes me not.   85

Cornwall

No more, perchance, does mine, nor his, nor hers.

Kent

Sir, 'tis my occupation to be plain:
I have seen better faces in my time
Than stands on any shoulder that I see
Before me at this instant.

Cornwall

                                    This is some fellow   90
Who, having been prais'd for bluntness, doth
    affect

55

A saucy roughness, and constrains the garb
Quite from his nature. He cannot flatter, he,
An honest mind and plain – he must speak
    truth.

95 An they will take it, so; if not, he's plain.
These kind of knaves I know, which in this
    plainness
Harbour more craft and more corrupter ends
Than twenty silly ducking observants
That stretch their duties nicely.

Kent

100 Sir, in good faith, in sincere verity,
Under th' allowance of your great aspect,
Whose influence, like the wreath of radiant fire
On flickering Phoebus' front –

Cornwall
                    What mean'st by this?

Kent

To go out of my dialect, which you discommend
so much. I know, sir, I am no flatterer. He that
beguil'd you in a plain accent was a plain knave;
which, for my part, I will not be, though I should
win your displeasure to entreat me to't.

Cornwall
What was th' offence you gave him?

Oswald
                    I never gave him any.

110 It pleas'd the King his master very late
To strike at me, upon his misconstruction;
When he, compact, and flattering his
    displeasure,
Tripp'd me behind; being down, insulted,
    rail'd,

115 And put upon him such a deal of man
That worthied him, got praises of the King
For him attempting who was self-subdu'd;
And in the fleshment of this dread exploit,
Drew on me here again.

Kent

> None of these rogues and cowards
> But Ajax is their fool.

Cornwall

>   Fetch forth the stocks.   120
> You stubborn ancient knave, you reverend
>   braggart,
> We'll teach you,

Kent

>   Sir, I am too old to learn.
> Call not your stocks for me; I serve the King,
> On whose employment I was sent to you.
> You shall do small respect, show too bold
>   malice
>   125
> Against the grace and person of my master,
> Stocking his messenger.

Cornwall

> Fetch forth the stocks. As I have life and
>   honour,
> There shall he sit till noon.

Regan

> Till noon! Till night, my lord; and all night too. 130

Kent

> Why, madam, if I were your father's dog,
> You should not use me so.

Regan

>   Sir, being his knave, I will.

Cornwall

> This is a fellow of the self-same colour
> Our sister speaks of. Come, bring away the
>   stocks. *[Stocks brought out.]*

Gloucester

> Let me beseech your Grace not to do so.   135
> His fault is much, and the good King his master
> Will check him for't; your purpos'd low
>   correction
> Is such as basest and contemned'st wretches
> For pilf'rings and most common trespasses

140 Are punish'd with. The King must take it ill
That he, so slightly valued in his messenger,
Should have him thus restrained.

Cornwall
                                        I'll answer that.

Regan
My sister may receive it much more worse
To have her gentleman abus'd, assaulted,
145 For following her affairs. Put in his legs.

[KENT is put in the stocks.]

Come, my good lord, away.

[Exeunt all but GLOUCESTER and KENT.]

Gloucester
I am sorry for thee, friend; 'tis the Duke's
    pleasure
Whose disposition, all the world well knows,
Will not be rubb'd nor stopp'd. I'll entreat for
    thee.

Kent
Pray, do not, sir. I have watch'd and travell'd
150   hard;
Some time I shall sleep out, the rest I'll whistle.
A good man's fortune may grow out at heels.
Give you good morrow!

Gloucester
                    The Duke's to blame in this;
'Twill be ill taken.

[Exit.]

Kent
Good King, that must approve the common
155   saw,
Thou out of heaven's benediction com'st
To the warm sun!
Approach, thou beacon to this under globe,
That by thy comfortable beams I may

Peruse this letter. Nothing almost sees miracles   160
But misery. I know 'tis from Cordelia,
Who hath most fortunately been inform'd
Of my obscured course. *[Reads]* '– and shall find
    time
From this enormous state – seeking to give
Losses their remedies.' All weary and
    o'er-watch'd,   165
Take vantage, heavy eyes, not to behold
This shameful lodging.
Fortune, good night: smile once more; turn thy
    wheel.

[He sleeps.]

Scene III.

The open country.

[Enter EDGAR.]

Edgar

I heard myself proclaim'd,
And by the happy hollow of a tree
Escap'd the hunt. No port is free; no place
That guard and most unusual vigilance
5   Does not attend my taking. Whiles I may scape
I will preserve myself; and am bethought
To take the basest and most poorest shape
That ever penury in contempt of man
Brought near to beast. My face I'll grime with
    filth,
10   Blanket my loins, elf all my hairs in knots,
And with presented nakedness outface
The winds and persecutions of the sky.
The country gives me proof and precedent
Of Bedlam beggars, who, with roaring voices,
15   Strike in their numb'd and mortified bare arms
Pins, wooden pricks, nails, sprigs of rosemary;
And with this horrible object, from low farms,
Poor pelting villages, sheep-cotes, and mills,
Sometimes with lunatic bans, sometime with
    prayers,
20   Enforce their charity. Poor Turlygod! poor Tom!
That's something yet. Edgar I nothing am.

[Exit.]

Scene IV.

Before Gloucester's castle.

[Enter LEAR, FOOL, *and* GENTLEMAN, *to* KENT *in the stocks.]*

Lear

'Tis strange that they should so depart from
  home,
And not send back my messenger.

Gentleman

As I learn'd,
The night before there was no purpose in them
Of this remove.

Kent

Hail to thee, noble master!

Lear

Ha!   5
Mak'st thou this shame thy pastime?

Kent

No, my lord.

Fool

Ha, ha! he wears cruel garters.
Horses are tied by the heads, dogs and bears by
th' neck, monkeys by th' loins, and men by th'
legs. When a man's over-lusty at legs, then he
wears wooden netherstocks.   10

Lear

What's he that hath so much thy place mistook
To set thee here?

Kent

It is both he and she,
Your son and daughter.

Lear

No.

Kent

Yes.   15

Lear

No, I say.

Kent
   I say, yea.
Lear
   No, no; they would not.
Kent
   Yes, they have.
20 *Lear*
   By Jupiter, I swear, no.
Kent
   By Juno, I swear, ay.
Lear
                  They durst not do't;
   They could not, would not do't; 'tis worse than
      murder
   To do upon respect such violent outrage.
   Resolve me with all modest haste which way
   Thou might'st deserve or they impose this
25   usage,
   Coming from us.
Kent
                  My lord, when at their home
   I did commend your Highness' letters to them,
   Ere I was risen from the place that show'd
   My duty kneeling, came there a reeking post,
   Stew'd in his haste, half breathless, panting
30   forth
   From Goneril his mistress salutations;
   Deliver'd letters, spite of intermission,
   Which presently they read; on whose contents
   They summon'd their meiny, straight took
      horse,
35 Commanded me to follow and attend
   The leisure of their answer, gave me cold looks;
   And meeting here the other messenger,
   Whose welcome I perceiv'd had poison'd mine,
   Being the very fellow which of late
40 Display'd so saucily against your Highness,
   Having more man than wit about me, drew.

He rais'd the house with loud and coward cries.
Your son and daughter found this trespass
    worth
The shame which here it suffers.

Fool

Winter's not gone yet, if the wild geese fly that   45
    way.
                Fathers that wear rags
                Do make their children blind;
                But fathers that bear bags
                Shall see their children kind.
                Fortune, that arrant whore,
                Ne'er turns the key to th' poor.
But, for all this, thou shalt have as many dolours
for thy daughters as thou canst tell in a year.

Lear

O, how this mother swells up toward my heart!   55
Hysterica passio – down, thou climbing sorrow,
Thy element's below. Where is this daughter?

Kent

With the earl, sir, here within.

Lear

                                        Follow me not;
Stay here.

                        [Exit.]

Gentleman

Made you no more offence but what you speak
of?   60

Kent

None.
How chance the King comes with so small a
    number?

Fool

An thou hadst been set i' th' stocks for that
question, thou'dst well deserv'd it.

Kent

Why, fool?   65

                                                                                    63

Fool

We'll set thee to school to an ant, to teach thee
there's no labouring i' th' winter. All that follow
their noses are led by their eyes but blind men;
and there's not a nose among twenty but can
smell him that's stinking. Let go thy hold when
a great wheel runs down a hill, lest it break thy
neck with following; but the great one that goes
upward, let him draw thee after. When a wise
man gives thee better counsel, give me mine
again. I would have none but knaves follow it,
75   since a fool gives it.

    That sir which serves and seeks for gain,
      And follows but for form,
    Will pack when it begins to rain,
      And leave thee in the storm.
80   But I will tarry; the fool will stay
      And let the wise man fly.
    The knave turns fool that runs away;
      The fool no knave, perdy.

Kent

Where learn'd you this, fool?

Fool

85   Not i' th' stocks, fool.

[Re-enter LEAR *and* GLOUCESTER.*]*

Lear

Deny to speak with me! They are sick! They are
    weary!
They have travell'd all the night! Mere fetches;
The images of revolt and flying off.
Fetch me a better answer.

Gloucester

                My dear lord,
90   You know the fiery quality of the Duke;
How unremovable and fix'd he is
In his own course.

Lear

Vengeance! plague! death! confusion!
Fiery? What quality? Why Gloucester,
   Gloucester,
I'd speak with the Duke of Cornwall and his
   wife.   95

Gloucester

Well, my good lord, I have inform'd them so.

Lear

Inform'd them! Dost thou understand me, man?

Gloucester

Ay, my good lord.

Lear

The King would speak with Cornwall; the dear
   father
Would with his daughter speak; commands
   their service.   100
Are they inform'd of this? My breath and blood!
Fiery? the fiery Duke? Tell the hot Duke that –
No, but not yet. May be he is not well.
Infirmity doth still neglect all office
Whereto our health is bound; we are not
   ourselves   105
When nature, being oppress'd, commands the
   mind
To suffer with the body. I'll forbear;
And am fallen out with my more headier will
To take the indispos'd and sickly fit
For the sound man. Death on my state!
   Wherefore   110
Should he sit here? This act persuades me
That this remotion of the Duke and her
Is practice only. Give me my servant forth.
Go tell the Duke and's wife I'd speak with them –
Now, presently. Bid them come forth and hear
   me,   115
Or at their chamber door I'll beat the drum
Till it cry sleep to death.

Gloucester
    I would have all well betwixt you.

    [Exit.]

Lear
119   O me, my heart, my rising heart! But, down.
Fool
    Cry to it, nuncle, as the cockney did to the eels
    when she put 'em i' th' paste alive; she knapp'd
    'em o' th' coxcombs with a stick, and cried 'Down,
    wantons, down'. 'Twas her brother that, in pure
124   kindness to his horse, butter'd his hay.

    *[Enter CORNWELL, REGAN, GLOUCESTER, and
    SERVANTS.]*

Lear
    Good morrow to you both.
Cornwall
                                    Hail to your Grace!

    [KENT here set at liberty.]

Regan
    I am glad to see your Highness.
Lear
    Regan, I think you are; I know what reason
    I have to think so. If thou shouldst not be glad,
    I would divorce me from thy mother's tomb,
    Sepulchring an adultress. *[To KENT]* O, are you
130   free?
    Some other time for that. – Beloved Regan,
    Thy sister's naught. O Regan, she hath tied
    Sharp-tooth'd unkindness, like a vulture, here.

    [Points to his heart.]

    I can scarce speak to thee; thou'lt not believe
135   With how deprav'd a quality – O Regan!
Regan
    I pray you, sir, take patience. I have hope

You less know how to value her desert
Than she to scant her duty.

Lear

Say, how is that?

Regan

I cannot think my sister in the least
Would fail her obligation. If, sir, perchance   140
She have restrain'd the riots of your followers,
'Tis on such ground, and to such wholesome
    end,
As clears her from all blame.

Lear

My curses on her!

Regan

O, sir, you are old;
Nature in you stands on the very verge   145
Of her confine. You should be rul'd and led
By some discretion that discerns your state
Better than you yourself. Therefore I pray you
That to our sister you do make return;
Say you have wrong'd her, sir.

Lear

Ask her forgiveness?   150
Do you but mark how this becomes the house:
'Dear daughter, I confess that I am old;

[Kneeling.]

Age is unnecessary; on my knees I beg
That you'll vouchsafe me raiment, bed, and
    food'.

Regan

Good sir, no more; these are unsightly tricks.   155
Return you to my sister.

Lear

[Rising] Never, Regan.
She hath abated me of half my train;
Look'd black upon me; struck me with her
    tongue,

67

Most serpent-like, upon the very heart.
160 All the stor'd vengeances of heaven fall
On her ingrateful top! Strike her young bones,
You taking airs, with lameness.

Cornwall
                Fie, sir, fie!

Lear
You nimble lightnings, dart your blinding
    flames
Into her scornful eyes. Infect her beauty,
165 You fen-suck'd fogs, drawn by the pow'rful sun
To fall and blast her pride.

Regan
                    O the blest gods!
So will you wish on me when the rash mood is
    on.

Lear
No, Regan, thou shalt never have my curse:
170 Thy tender-hefted nature shall not give
Thee o'er to harshness. Her eyes are fierce, but
    thine
Do comfort and not burn. 'Tis not in thee
To grudge my pleasures, to cut off my train,
To bandy hasty words, to scant my sizes,
175 And, in conclusion, to oppose the bolt
Against my coming in; thou better know'st
The offices of nature, bond of childhood,
Effects of courtesy, dues of gratitude;
Thy half o' th' kingdom hast thou not forgot,
Wherein I thee endow'd.

Regan
180   Good sir, to th' purpose.

Lear
Who put my man i' th' stocks?

[Tucket within.]

Cornwall
                What trumpet's that?

Regan
    I know't – my sister's. This approves her letter,
    That she would soon be here.

              [Enter OSWALD*]*

              Is your lady come?
Lear
    This is a slave whose easy-borrow'd pride
    Dwells in the fickle grace of her he follows.   185
    Out, varlet, from my sight!
Cornwall
                  What means your Grace?

            [Enter GONERIL.*]*

Lear
    Who stock'd my servant? Regan. I have good
       hope
    Thou didst not know on't. – Who comes here?
       O heavens,
    If you do love old men, if your sweet sway
    Allow obedience, if you yourselves are old,   190
    Make it your cause; send down, and take my
       part.
    [To GONERIL*]* Art not asham'd to look upon this
       beard? –
    O Regan, will you take her by the hand?
Goneril
    Why not by th' hand, sir? How have I
       offended?
    All's not offence that indiscretion finds,   195
    And dotage terms so.
Lear
               O sides, you are too tough!
    Will you yet hold? – How came my man i' th'
       stocks?
Cornwall
    I set him there, sir; but his own disorders.
    Deserv'd much less advancement.

Lear

You! did you?

Regan

200   I pray you, father, being weak, seem so.
If, till the expiration of your month,
You will return and sojourn with my sister,
Dismissing half your train, come then to me.
I am now from home, and out of that provision

205   Which shall be needful for your entertainment.

Lear

Return to her, and fifty men dismiss'd?
No, rather I abjure all roofs, and choose
To wage against the enmity o' th' air,
To be a comrade with the wolf and owl –

210   Necessity's sharp pinch! Return with her?
Why, the hot-blooded France, that dowerless took
Our youngest born – I could as well be brought
To knee his throne, and, squire-like, pension beg
To keep base life afoot. Return with her?

215   Persuade me rather to be slave and sumpter
To this detested groom. *[Pointing to* OSWALD.*]*

Goneril

At your choice, sir.

Lear

I prithee, daughter, do not make me mad.
I will not trouble thee, my child; farewell.
We'll no more meet, no more see one another.
But yet thou art my flesh, my blood, my

220   daughter;
Or rather a disease that's in my flesh,
Which I must needs call mine; thou art a boil,
A plague-sore, or embossed carbuncle
In my corrupted blood. But I'll not chide thee;

225   Let shame come when it will, I do not call it;
I do not bid the Thunder-bearer shoot,

Nor tell tales of thee to high-judging Jove,
Mend when thou canst; be better at thy leisure;
I can be patient; I can stay with Regan,
I and my hundred knights.   230

Regan

                    Not altogether so.
I look'd not for you yet, nor am provided
For your fit welcome. Give ear, sir, to my sister;
For those that mingle reason with your passion
Must be content to think you old, and so –
But she knows what she does.

Lear

                    Is this well spoken? 235

Regan

I dare avouch it, sir. What, fifty followers?
Is it not well? What should you need of more?
Yea, or so many, sith that both charge and
   danger
Speak 'gainst so great a number? How in one
   house
Should many people under two commands   240
Hold amity? 'Tis hard; almost impossible.

Goneril

Why might not you, my lord, receive
   attendance
From those that she calls servants, or from
   mine?

Regan

Why not, my lord? If then they chanc'd to
   slack ye,
We could control them. If you will come to me – 245
For now I spy a danger – I entreat you
To bring but five and twenty. To no more
Will I give place or notice.

Lear

I gave you all.

Regan

              And in good time you gave it.

Lear

250   Made you my guardians, my depositaries;
But kept a reservation to be followed
With such a number. What, must I come to
    you
With five and twenty, Regan? Said you so?

Regan

And speak't again, my lord. No more with me.

Lear

Those wicked creatures yet do look
255   well-favour'd
When others are more wicked; not being the
    worst.
Stands in some rank of praise. *[To* GONERIL*]* I'll
    go with thee.
Thy fifty yet doth double five and twenty,
And thou art twice her love.

Goneril

                Hear me, my lord:
260   What need you five and twenty, ten, or five,
To follow in a house where twice so many
Have a command to tend you?

Regan

                  What need one?

Lear

O, reason not the need! Our basest beggars
Are in the poorest thing superfluous.
265   Allow not nature more than nature needs,
Man's life is cheap as beast's. Thou art a lady;
If only to go warm were gorgeous,
Why, nature needs not what thou gorgeous
    wear'st.
Which scarcely keeps thee warm. But, for true
    need –
You heavens, give me that patience, patience I
270   need.
You see me here, you gods, a poor old man.
As full of grief as age; wretched in both.

If it be you that stirs these daughters' hearts
Against their father, fool me not so much
To bear it tamely; touch me with noble anger, 275
And let not women's weapons, water-drops,
Stain my man's cheeks! No, you unnatural
        hags,
I will have such revenges on you both
That all the world shall – I will do such things –
What they are yet I know not; but they shall
        be
The terrors of the earth. You think I'll weep. 280
No, I'll not weep. *[Storm and tempest.]*
I have full cause of weeping; but this heart
Shall break into a hundred thousand flaws
Or ere I'll weep. O fool, I shall go mad! 285

        [Exeunt LEAR, GLOUCESTER, KENT, *and* FOOL.*]*

Cornwall
    Let us withdraw; 'twill be a storm.
Regan
    This house is little: the old man and's people
    Cannot be well bestow'd.
Goneril
    'Tis his own blame; hath put himself from rest,
    And must needs taste his folly. 290
Regan
    For his particular, I'll receive him gladly,
    But not one follower.
Goneril
                    So am I purpos'd.
    Where is my Lord of Glouscester?
Cornwall
    Followed the old man forth.

                [Re-enter GLOUCESTER.*]*

                He is return'd.
Gloucester
    The King is in high rage.

Cornwall

295   Whither is he going?

Gloucester

He calls to horse; but will I know not whither.

Cornwall

'Tis best to give him way; he leads himself.

Goneril

My Lord, entreat him by no means to stay.

Gloucester

Alack, the night comes on, and the high winds

300   Do sorely ruffle: for many miles about

There's scarce a bush.

Regan

O sir, to wilful men

The injuries that they themselves procure

Must be their schoolmasters. Shut up your
       doors.

He is attended with a desperate train;

305   And what they may incense him to, being apt

To have his ear abus'd, wisdom bids fear.

Cornwall

Shut up your doors, my lord; 'tis a wild night.

My Regan counsels well. Come out o' th' storm.

[Exeunt.]

ACT THREE
Scene I.

A heath.

[Storm still. Enter KENT *and a* GENTLEMAN, *severally.]*

Kent

Who's there, besides foul weather?

Gentleman

One minded like the weather, most unquietly.

Kent

I know you. Where's the King?

Gentleman

Contending with the fretful elements;
Bids the wind blow the earth into the sea,   5
Or swell the curled waters 'bove the main,
That things might change or cease: tears his
    white hair,
Which the impetuous blasts, with eyeless rage,
Catch in their fury, and make nothing of;
Strives in his little world of man to out-scorn   10
The to-and-fro conflicting wind and rain.
This night, wherein the cub-drawn bear would
    couch,
The lion and the belly-pinched wolf
Keep their fur dry, unbonneted he runs,
And bids what will take all.

Kent

                 But who is with him?   15

Gentleman

None but the fool; who labours to out-jest
His heart-struck injuries.

Kent

            Sir, I do know you,
And dare, upon the warrant of my note,
Commend a dear thing to you. There is division,

20   Although as yet the face of it be cover'd
         With mutual cunning, 'twixt Albany and
            Cornwall;
         Who have – as who have not that their great
            stars
         Thron'd and set high? – servants, who seem no
            less,
         Which are to France the spies and speculations
25   Intelligent of our state. What hath been seen.
         Either in snuffs and packings of the Dukes;
         Or the hard rein which both of them hath
            borne
         Against the old kind King; or something deeper.
         Whereof perchance these are but furnishings –
30   But true it is from France there comes a power
         Into this scatter'd kingdom, who already,
         Wise in our negligence, have secret feet
         In some of our best ports, and are at point
         To show their open banner. Now to you;
35   If on my credit you dare build so far
         To make your speed to Dover, you shall find
         Some that will thank you making just report
         Of how unnatural and bemadding sorrow
         The King hath cause to plain.
40   I am a gentleman of blood and breeding;
         And from some knowledge and assurance offer
         This office to you.
Gentleman
         I will talk further with you.
   Kent
                              No, do not.
         For confirmation that I am much more
45   Than my out-wall, open this purse and take
         What it contains. If you shall see Cordelia,
         As fear not but you shall, show her this ring;
         And she will tell you who your fellow is
         That yet you do not know. Fie on this storm!
50   I will go seek the King.

Gentleman

Give me your hand. Have you no more to say?

Kent

Few words, but to effect, more than all yet;
That when we have found the King – in which your pain
That way, I'll this – he that first lights on him
Holla the other.   55

[Exeunt severally.]

Scene II.

Another part of the heath.

[Storm still. Enter LEAR and FOOL.]

Lear

Blow, winds, and crack your cheeks; rage, blow.
You cataracts and hurricanoes, spout
Till you have drench'd our steeples, drown'd
the cocks.
You sulph'rous and thought-executing fires,
5 Vaunt-couriers of oak-cleaving thunder-bolts,
Singe my white head. And thou, all-shaking
thunder,
Strike flat the thick rotundity o' th' world;
Crack nature's moulds, all germens spill at
once,
That makes ingrateful man.

Fool

10 O nuncle, court holy water in a dry house is better
than this rain-water out o' door. Good nuncle,
in; ask thy daughters' blessing. Here's a night
pities neither wise men nor fools.

Lear

Rumble thy bellyful. Spit, fire; spout, rain.
15 Nor rain, wind, thunder, fire, are my daughters.
I tax not you, you elements, with unkindness:
I never gave you kingdom, call'd you children;
You owe me no subscription. Then let fall
Your horrible pleasure. Here I stand, your slave,
20 A poor, infirm, weak and despis'd old man:
But yet I call you servile ministers
That will with two pernicious daughters join
Your high-engender'd battles 'gainst a head
So old and white as this. O, ho! 'tis foul!

Fool

25 He that has a house to put's head in has a good
head-piece.

The cod-piece that will house
Before the head has any,
The head and he shall louse;
So beggars marry many.   30
The man that makes his toe
What he his heart should make
Shall of a corn cry woe,
And turn his sleep to wake.
For there was never yet fair woman but she made   35
mouths in a glass.

[Enter KENT.*]*

Lear

No, I will be the pattern of all patience; I will say
nothing.

Kent

Who's there?

Fool

Marry, here's grace and a cod-piece; that's a wise   40
man and a fool.

Kent

Alas, sir, are you here? Things that love night
Love not such nights as these; the wrathful
skies
Gallow the very wanderers of the dark
And make them keep their caves. Since I was
man   45
Such sheets of fire, such bursts of horrid
thunder,
Such groans of roaring wind and rain, I never
Remember to have heard. Man's nature cannot
carry
Th' affliction nor the fear.

Lear

                    Let the great gods,
That keep this dreadful pudder o'er our heads,   50
Find out their enemies now. Tremble, thou
wretch,

79

That hast within thee undivulged crimes
Unwhipp'd of justice. Hide thee, thou bloody
    hand;
Thou perjur'd, and thou simular man of virtue
55 That art incestuous; caitiff, to pieces shake,
That under covert and convenient seeming
Hast practis'd on man's life. Close pent-up
    guilts,
Rive your concealing continents, and cry
These dreadful summoners grace. I am a man
60 More sinn'd against than sinning.

Kent

                    Alack, bare-headed!
Gracious my lord, hard by here is a hovel;
Some friendship will it lend you 'gainst the
    tempest.
Repose you there, while I to this hard house –
More harder than the stones whereof 'tis rais'd;
65 Which even but now, demanding after you,
Denied me to come in – return, and force
Their scanted courtesy.

Lear

                    My wits begin to turn.
Come on, my boy. How dost, my boy? Art
    cold?
I am cold myself. Where is this straw, my
    fellow?
70 The art of our necessities is strange
That can make vile things precious. Come, your
    hovel.
Poor fool and knave, I have one part in my
    heart
That's sorry yet for thee.

Fool

[Sings] He that has and a little tiny wit
75 With heigh-ho, the wind and the rain –
Must make content with his fortunes fit,
Though the rain it raineth every day.

80

Lear
> True, my good boy. Come, bring us to this hovel.

[Exeunt LEAR and KENT.]

Fool
> This is a brave night to cool a courtezan. I'll
>   speak a prophecy ere I go.   80
> When priests are more in word than matter;
> When brewers mar their malt with water;
> When nobles are their tailors' tutors;
> No heretics burn'd, but wenches' suitors;
> When every case in law is right;   85
> No squire in debt, nor no poor knight;
> When slanders do not live in tongues;
> Nor cutpurses come not to throngs;
> When usurers tell their gold i'; th' field;
> And bawds and whores do churches build –   90
> Then shall the realm of Albion
> Come to great confusion.
> Then comes the time, who lives to see't,
> That going shall be us'd with feet.
> This prophecy Merlin shall make, for I live   95
>   before his time.

[Exit.]

Scene III.

Gloucester's castle.

[Enter GLOUCESTER *and* EDMUND.*]*

Gloucester

Alack, alack, Edmund, I like not this unnatural
dealing. When I desired their leave that I might
pity him, they took from me the use of mine own
house, charg'd me, on pain of perpetual displeasure,
neither to speak of him, entreat for him, or any
6   way sustain him.

Edmund

Most savage and unnatural!

Gloucester

Go to; say you nothing. There is division between
the Dukes; and a worse matter than that. I have
received a letter this night – 'tis dangerous to be
spoken; I have lock'd the letter in my closet. These
injuries the King now bears will be revenged home;
there is part of a power already footed. We must
incline to the King. I will look him, and privily
relieve him. Go you and maintain talk with the
Duke, that my charity be not of him perceived; if
he ask for me. I am ill, and gone to bed. If I die
for it, as no less is threatened me, the King my
old master must be relieved. There is strange things
toward, Edmund; pray you be careful.

[Exit.]

Edmund

21   This courtesy forbid thee shall the Duke
Instantly know, and of that letter too.
This seems a fair deserving, and must draw me
That which my father loses – no less than all.
The younger rises, when the old doth fall.

[Exit.]

Scene IV.

Before a hovel on the heath.

[Storm still, Enter LEAR, KENT, *and* FOOL.*]*

Kent

    Here is the place, my lord; good my lord, enter.
    The tyranny of the open night's too rough
    For nature to endure.

Lear

               Let me alone.

Kent

    Good my lord, enter here.

Lear

                 Wilt break my heart?   5

Kent

    I had rather break mine own. Good my lord, enter.

Lear

    Thou think'st 'tis much that this contentious
        storm
    Invades us to the skin; so 'tis to thee,
    But where the greater malady is fix'd,
    The lesser is scarce felt. Thou'dst shun a bear;
    But if thy flight lay toward the roaring sea,   10
    Thou'dst meet the bear i' th' mouth. When the
        mind's free
    The body's delicate; this tempest in my mind
    Doth from my senses take all feeling else,
    Save what beats there. Filial ingratitude!
    Is it not as this mouth should tear this hand   15
    For lifting food to't? But I will punish home.
    No, I will weep no more. In such a night,
    To shut me out! Pour on; I will endure.
    In such a night as this! O Regan, Goneril!
    Your old kind father, whose frank heart gave
        all!
                          20
    O, that way madness lies; let me shun that;
    No more of that.

Kent

> Good my lord, enter here.

Lear

> Prithee go in thyself; seek thine own ease.
> This tempest will not give me leave to ponder
> On things would hurt me more. But I'll go in.
> *[To the Fool]* In, boy; go first – You house-less
>   poverty –
> Nay, get thee in. I'll pray, and then I'll sleep.

25

> *[Exit* FOOL.*]*

> Poor naked wretches, wheresoe'er you are.
> That bide the pelting of this pitiless storm.
> How shall your houseless heads and unfed
>   sides.
> Your loop'd and window'd raggedness, defend
>   you
> From seasons such as these? O, I have ta'en
> Too little care of this! Take physic, pomp;
> Expose thyself to feel what wretches feel,
> That thou mayst shake the superflux to them,
> And show the heavens more just.

30

35

Edgar

> *[Within]* Fathom and half, fathom and half! Poor
> Tom!

> *[Enter* FOOL *from the hovel.]*

Fool

> Come not in here, nuncle, here's a spirit.
> Help me, help me!

40

Kent

> Give me thy hand. Who's there?

Fool

> A spirit, a spirit. He says his name's poor Tom.

Kent

> What art thou that dost grumble there i' th'
>   straw?
> Come forth.

[Enter EDGAR, disguised as a madman.]

Edgar

Away! the foul fiend follows me. 45

Through the sharp hawthorn blows the cold
wind.

Humh! go to thy cold bed and warm thee.

Lear

Didst thou give all to thy daughters? And art thou
come to this? 49

Edgar

Who gives anything to poor Tom? whom the foul
fiend hath led through fire and through flame,
through ford and whirlpool, o'er bog and quagmire;
that hath laid knives under his pillow and halters
in his pew, set ratsbane by his porridge; made him
proud of heart, to ride on a bay trotting-horse over
four-inched bridges, to course his own shadow for
a trailor. Bless thy five wits! Tom's a-cold. O, do de,
do de, do de. Bless thee from whirlwinds, star-
blasting, and taking! Do poor Tom some charity,
whom the foul fiend vexes. There could I have him
now – and there – and there again – and there.

[Storm still.]

Lear

What, has his daughters brought him to this
pass?

Could'st thou save nothing? Would'st thou give
'em all?

Fool

Nay, he reserv'd a blanket, else we had been all
sham'd. 65

Lear

Now all the plagues that in the pendulous air
Hang fated o'er men's faults light on thy
daughters!

Kent

he hath no daughters, sir.

Lear
> Death, traitor! Nothing could have subdu'd
> nature
> To such a lowness but his unkind daughters.
> Is it the fashion that discarded fathers
> Should have thus little mercy on their flesh?
> Judicious punishment! 'twas this flesh begot
> Those pelican daughters.

70

Edgar
> Pillicock sat on Pillicock-hill. Alow, alow, loo,
> loo!

75

Fool
> This cold night will turn us all to fools and
> madmen.

Edgar
> Take heed o' th' foul fiend; obey thy parents; keep
> thy words justly; swear not; commit not with
> man's sworn spouse; set not thy sweet heart on
> proud array. Tom's a-cold.

80

Lear
> What hast thou been?

Edgar
> A serving-man, proud in heart and mind; that
> curl'd my hair; wore gloves in my cap; serv'd the
> lust of my mistress' heart, and did the act of
> darkness with her; swore as many oaths as I spake
> words, and broke them in the sweet face of
> heaven; one that slept in the contriving of lust,
> and wak'd to do it. Wine lov'd I deeply, dice
> dearly; and in woman out-paramour'd the Turk.
> False of heart, light of ear, bloody of hand; hog
> in sloth, fox in stealth, wolf in greediness, dog in
> madness, lion in prey. Let not the creaking of
> shoes nor the rustling of silks betray thy poor
> heart to woman. Keep thy foot out of brothels,
> thy hand out of plackets, thy pen from lenders'
> books, and defy the foul fiend.
> Still through the hawthorn blows the cold wind.

96

Says suum, mun, nonny.
Dolphin my boy, boy, sessa! let him trot by.

[Storm still.]

Lear

Why, thou wert better in a grave than to answer
with thy uncover'd body this extremity of the
skies. Is man no more than this? Consider him
well. Thou ow'st the worm no silk, the beast no
hide, the sheep no wool, the cat no perfume. Ha!
here's three on's are sophisticated! Thou art the
thing itself: unaccommodated man is no more
but such a poor, bare, forked animal as thou art.
Off, off, you lendings! Come, unbutton here.   108
[Tearing off his clothes.]

[Enter GLOUCESTER *with a torch.]*

Fool

Prithee, nuncle, be contented; 'tis a naughty night
to swim in. Now a little fire in a wild field were
like an old lecher's heart – a small spark, all the
rest on's body cold. Look, here comes a walking
fire.   112

Edgar

This is the foul fiend Flibbertigibbet; he begins at
curfew, and walks till the first cock; he gives the
web and the pin, squences the eye, and makes
the hare-lip; mildews the white wheat, and hurts
the poor creature of earth.   117

 Swithold footed thrice the 'old;
 He met the nightmare and her nine-fold;
 Bid her alight   120
 And her troth plight,
 And aroint thee, witch, aroint thee!

Kent

How fares your Grace?

Lear

What's he?

Kent

125   Who's there? What is't you seek?

Gloucester

What are you there? Your names?

Edgar

Poor Tom; that eats the swimming frog, the toad, the tadpole, the wall-newt, and the water; that in the fury of his heart, when the foul fiend rages, eats cow-dung for sallets, swallows the old rat and the ditch-dog, drinks the green mantle of the standing pool; who is whipp'd from tithing to tithing, and stock-punish'd, and imprison'd; who hath had three suits to his back, six shirts to his body – Horse to ride, and weapon to wear; But mice and rats, and such small deer,

136   Have been Tom's food for seven long year,
Beware my follower. Peace, Smulkin; peace, thou fiend!

Gloucester

What, hath your Grace no better company?

Edgar

The prince of darkness is a gentleman;

140   Modo he's call'd, and Mahu.

Gloucester

Our flesh and blood, my lord, is grown so vile
That it doth hate what gets it.

Edgar

Poor Tom's a-cold.

Gloucester

Go in with me: my duty cannot suffer

145   T' obey in all your daughters' hard commands.
Though their injunction be to bar my doors,
And let this tyrannous night take hold upon you,
Yet have I ventur'd to come seek you out,
And bring you where both fire and food is ready.

Lear

First let me talk with this philosopher.   150
What is the cause of thunder?

Kent

Good my lord, take this offer; go into th' house.

Lear

I'll talk a word with this same learned Theban.
What is your study?

Edgar

How to prevent the fiend and to kill vermin.   155

Lear

Let me ask you one word in private.

Kent

Importune him once more to go, my lord;
His wits begin t' unsettle.

[Storm still.]

Gloucester

                        Canst thou blame him?
His daughters seek his death. Ah, that good
      Kent! –
He said it would be thus – poor, banish'd man!   160
Thou sayest the King grows mad; I'll tell thee,
      friend,
I am almost mad myself. I had a son,
Now outlaw'd from my blood; he sought my life
But lately, very late. I lov'd him, friend –
No father his son dearer. True to tell thee,   165
The grief hath craz'd my wits. What a night's
      this!
I do beseech your Grace –

Lear

                        O, cry you mercy, sir.
Noble philosopher, your company.

Edgar

Tom's a-cold.

Gloucester

In, fellow, there, into th'hovel; keep thee warm. 170

Lear
Come, let's in all.

Kent
                This way, my lord.

Lear
                          With him;
I will keep still with my philosopher.

Kent
Good my lord, soothe him; let him take the fellow.

Gloucester
Take him you on.

Kent
175   Sirrah, come on; go along with us.

Lear
Come, good Athenian.

Gloucester
No words, no words! Hush.

Edgar
Child Rowland to the dark tower came,
His word was still 'Fie, foh, and fum,
I smell the blood of a British man'.

               [Exeunt.]

Scene V.

Gloucester's castle.

[Enter CORNWALL *and* EDMUND.*]*

Cornwall

I will have my revenge ere I depart his house.

Edmund

How, my lord, I may be censured, that nature thus gives way to loyalty, something fears me to think of.

Cornwall

I now perceive it was not altogether your brother's evil disposition made him seek his death; but a provoking merit, set a-work by a reprovable badness in himself.   7

Edmund

How malicious is my fortune, that I must repent to be just! This is the letter he spoke of, which approves him an intelligent party to the advantages of France. O heavens! that this treason were not, or not I the detector!   12

Cornwall

Go with me to the Duchess.

Edgar

If the matter of this paper be certain, you have mighty business in hand.

Cornwall

True or false, it hath made thee Earl of Gloucester. Seek out where thy father is, that he may be ready for our apprehension.   18

Edmund

[Aside] If I find him comforting the King, it will stuff his suspicion more fully. – I will persever in my course of loyalty, though the conflict be sore between that and my blood.   22

Cornwall

I will lay trust upon thee; and thou shalt find a dearer father in my love.

[Exeunt.]

Scene VI.

An outhouse of Gloucester's castle.

[Enter KENT and GLOUCESTER.]

Gloucester
Here is better than the open air; take it thankfully.
I will piece out the comfort with what addition
I can, I will not be long from you.   3

Kent
All the pow'r of his wits have given way to his
impatience. The gods reward your kindness!

[Exit Gloucester.]

[Enter LEAR, EDGAR, and Fool.]

Edgar
Fraterretto calls me, and tells me Nero is an angler
in the lake of darkness. Pray, innocent, and beware
the foul fiend.

Fool
Prithee, nuncle, tell me whether a madman be a
gentleman or a yeoman?   10

Lear
A king, a king!

Fool
No; he's a yeoman that has a gentleman to his
son; for he's a mad yeoman that sees his son a
gentleman before him.

Lear
To have a thousand with red burning spits Come   15
hizzing in upon 'em –

Edgar
The foul fiends bites my back.

Fool
He's mad that trusts in the tameness of a wolf, a
horse's health, a boy's love, or a whore's oath.

Lear

20   It shall be done; I will arraign them straight.
     [To EDGAR*]* Come, sit thou here, most learned
          justicer.
     [To the FOOL*]* Thou, sapient sir, sit here. – Now,
          you she-foxes!

Edgar

     Look where he stands and glares!
     Want'st thou eyes at trial, madam?
25   Come o'er the bourn, Bessy, to me.

Fool

     Her boat hath a leak,
     And she must not speak,
     Why she dares not come over to thee.

Edgar

     The foul fiend haunts poor Tom in the voice of
     a nightingale. Hoppedance cries in Tom's belly
     for two white herring. Croak not, black angel; I
32   have no food for thee.

Kent

     How do you, sir? Stand you not so amaz'd.
     Will you lie down and rest upon the
          cushions?

Lear

35   I'll see their trial first. Bring in their evidence.
     [To EDGAR*]* Thou robed man of justice, take thy
          place.
     [To the FOOL*]* And thou, his yoke-fellow of equity,
     Bench by his side. *[To* KENT*]* You are o' th'
          commission,
     Sit you too.

Edgar

40   Let us deal justly.
     Sleepest or wakest thou, jolly shepherd?
     Thy sheep be in the corn,
     And for one blast of thy minikin mouth,
     Thy sheep shall take no harm.
45   Pur! the cat is grey.

Lear

Arraign her first; 'tis Goneril. I here take my oath
before this honourable assembly she kick'd the
poor King her father.

Fool

Come hither, mistress. Is your name Goneril?

Lear

She cannot deny it.

Fool   50

Cry you mercy, I took you for a joint-stool.

Lear

And here's another, whose warp'd looks proclaim
What store her heart is made on. Stop her there!
Arms, arms, sword, fire! Corruption in the place!
False justicer, why hast thou let her scape?   55

Edgar

Bless thy five wits!

Kent

O pity! Sir, where is the patience now
That you so oft have boasted to retain?

Edgar

[Aside] My tears begin to take his part so much
They mar my counterfeiting.   60

Lear

The little dogs and all,
Tray, Blanch, and Sweetheart, see, they bark at
me.

Edgar

Tom will throw his head at them.
Avaunt, you curs!
Be thy mouth or black or white,   65
Tooth that poisons if it bite;
Mastiff, greyhound, mongrel grim,
Hound or spaniel, brach or lym,
Or bobtail tike or trundle-tail –
Tom will make him weep and wail;   70
For, with throwing thus my head,
Dogs leapt the hatch, and all are fled.

Do de, de, de. Sessa! Come, march to wakes and
fairs and market-towns. Poor Tom, thy horn is
74   dry.

Lear

Then let them anatomize Regan; see what breeds
about her heart. Is there any cause in nature that
make these hard hearts? *[To* EDGAR*]*
You, sir, I entertain for one of my hundred; only
I do not like the fashion of your garments. You
80   will say they are Persian, but let them be chang'd.

Kent

Now, good my lord, lie here and rest awhile.

Lear

Make no noise, make no noise; draw the curtains.
So, so. We'll go to supper i' th' morning.

Fool

85   And I'll go to bed at noon.

[Re-enter GLOUCESTER.*]*

Gloucester

Come hither, friend. Where is the King my
master?

Kent

Here, sir; but trouble him not – his wits are
gone.

Gloucester

Good friend, I prithee, take him in thy arms;
I have o'erheard a plot of death upon him.
90   There is a litter ready; lay him in't
And drive toward Dover, friend, where thou
    shalt meet
Both welcome and protection. Take up thy
    master;
If thou shouldst dally half an hour, his life,
With thine, and all that offer to defend him,
95   Stand in assured loss. Take up, take up;
And follow me, that will to some provision
Give thee quick conduct.

Kent

                        Oppressed nature sleeps.
This rest might yet have balm'd thy broken
    sinews,
Which, if convenience will not allow,
Stand in hard cure, *[To the Fool]* Come, help to
    bear thy master;   100
Thou must not stay behind.

Gloucester

                       Come, come, away.

[Exeunt all but EDGAR.*]*

Edgar

When we our betters see bearing our woes,
We scarcely think our miseries our foes.
Who alone suffers suffers most i' th' mind,
Leaving free things and happy shows behind;   105
But then the mind much sufferance doth
    o'erskip
When grief hath mates, and bearing fellowship.
How light and portable my pain seems now,
When that which makes me bend makes the
    King bow –
He childed as I father'd! Tom, away!   110
Mark the high noises; and thyself bewray,
When false opinion, whose wrong thoughts
    defile thee,
In thy just proof repeals and reconciles thee.
What will hap more to-night, safe scape the
    King!
Lurk, lurk.   115

[Exit.]

Scene VII.

Gloucester's castle.

[Enter CORNWALL, GONERIL, EDMUND, *and* SERVANTS.]

Cornwall

[To GONERIL] Post speedily to my lord your
husband; show him this letter. The army of France
is landed. – Seek out the traitor Gloucester.

[Exeunt some of the SERVANTS.]*

Regan

Hang him instantly.

Goneril

5 Pluck out his eyes.

Cornwall

Leave him to my displeasure.
Edmund, keep you our sister company. The
revenges we are bound to take upon your
traitorous father are not fit for your beholding.
Advise the Duke, where you are going, to a most
festinate preparation; we are bound to the like.
Our posts shall be swift and intelligent betwixt us.
Farewell, dear sister; farewell, my Lord of Gloucester.

[Enter OSWALD.]

How now! where's the King?

Oswald

My Lord of Gloucester hath convey'd him
hence.

15 Some five or six and thirty of his knights,
Hot questrists after him, met him at gate;
Who, with some other of the lord's dependants,
Are gone with him toward Dover, where they
boast
To have well-armed friends.

Cornwall

Get horses for your mistress.

Goneril
    Farewell, sweet lord, and sister.   20
Cornwall
    Edmund, farewell.

    [Exeunt GONERIL, EDMUND, *and* OSWALD.*]*

                Go seek the traitor Gloucester,
Pinion him like a thief, bring him before us.

    [Exeunt other SERVANTS.*]*

Though well we may not pass upon his life
Without the form of justice, yet our power
Shall do a court'sy to our wrath, which men
May blame, but not control.

    [Enter GLOUCESTER, *brought in by two or three.]*

                Who's there? the traitor?
Regan
    Ingrateful fox! 'tis he.   27
Cornwall
    Bind fast his corky arms.
Gloucester
    What means your Graces? Good my friends,
      consider
    You are my guests; do me no foul play, friends.   30
Cornwall
    Bind him, I say. [SERVANTS *bind him.*]
Regan
                Hard, hard. O filthy traitor!
Gloucester
    Unmerciful lady as you are, I'm none.
Cornwall
    To this chair bind him. Villain, thou shalt find –

    *[*REGAN *plucks his beard.}*

Gloucester
    By the kind gods, 'tis most ignobly done
    To pluck me by the beard.   35

Regan
 So white, and such a traitor!
Gloucester
                                        Naughty lady,
 These hairs which thou dost ravish from my
   chin
 Will quicken and accuse thee. I am your host.
 With robbers' hands my hospitable favours
40 You should not ruffle thus. What will you do?
Cornwall
 Come, sir, what letters had you late from France?
Regan
 Be simple-answer'd, for we know the truth.
Cornwall
 And what confederacy have you with the traitors
 Late footed in the kingdom?
Regan To whose hands you have sent the lunatic
45   King:
 Speak.
Gloucester
 I have a letter guessingly set down,
 Which came from one that's of a neutral heart,
 And not from one oppos'd.
Cornwall
                                        Cunning.
Regan
                                        And false.
Cornwall
 Where hast thou sent the King?
Gloucester
                                        To Dover.
50
Regan
 Wherefore to Dover? Wast thou not charg'd at
   peril –
Cornwall
 Wherefore to Dover? Let him first answer that.
Gloucester
 I am tied to the stake, and I must stand the course.

Regan
  Wherefore to Dover?
Gloucester
  Because I would not see thy cruel nails   55
  Pluck out his poor old eyes; nor thy fierce sister
  In his anointed flesh rash boarish fangs.
  The sea, with such a storm as his bare head
  In hell-black night endur'd, would have buoy'd
    up
  And quench'd the stelled fires.   60
  Yet, poor old heart, he holp the heavens to
    rain.
  If wolves had at thy gate howl'd that dern
    time,
  Thou shouldst have said 'Good porter, turn the
    key'.
  All cruels else subscribe, but I shall see
  The winged vengeance overtake such children.   65
Cornwall
  See't shalt thou never. Fellows, hold the chair.
  Upon these eyes of thine I'll set my foot.
Gloucester
  He that will think to live till he be old,
  Give me some help! – O cruel! O you gods!
Regan
  One side will mock another; th' other too.   70
Cornwall
  If you see vengeance –
1 Servant
                        Hold your hand, my lord.
  I have serv'd you ever since I was a child;
  But better service have I never done you,
  Than now to bid you hold.
Regan
                          How now, you dog!
1 Servant
  If you did wear a beard upon your chin   75
  I'd shake it on this quarrel. What do you mean?

Cornwall
My villain!

[*They draw and fight.*]

1 Servant
Nay, then come on, and take the chance of
anger.

[CORNWALL *is wounded.*]

Regan
Give me thy sword. A peasant stand up thus!

[*She takes a sword and stabs him from behind.*]

1 Servant
80   O, I am slain! My lord, you have one eye left
To see some mischief on him. O!

[*Dies.*]

Cornwall
Lest it see more, prevent it. Out vile jelly!
Where is thy lustre now?

Gloucester
All dark and comfortless! Where's my son
Edmund?
85   Edmund, enkindle all the sparks of nature
To quit this horrid act.

Regan
                Out, trecherous villain!
Thou call'st on him that hates thee. It was he
That made the overture of thy treasons to us;
Who is too good to pity thee.

Gloucester
90   O my follies! Then Edgar was abus'd.
Kind gods, forgive me that, and prosper him.

Regan
Go thrust him out at gates and let him smell
His way to Dover.

[GLOUCESTER *led out.*]

How is't my lord? How look you?

Cornwall
I have receiv'd a hurt. Follow me, lady.
Turn out that eyeless villain; throw this slave   95
Upon the dunghill. Regan, I bleed apace.
Untimely comes this hurt. Give me your arm.

[Exit CORNWALL, led by REGAN.]

2 Servant
I'll never care what wickedness I do,
If this man come to good.

3 Servant
                              If she live long,
And in the end meet the old course of death,   100
Women will all turn monsters.

2 Servant
Let's follow the old Earl and get the Bedlam
To lead him where he would. His roguish
          madness
Allows itself to anything.

3 Servant
Go thou. I'll fetch some flax and whites of eggs   105
To apply to his bleeding face. Now heaven help
          him!

[Exeunt.]

ACT FOUR
Scene I.

The Heath.

[Enter EDGAR.]

Edgar
Yet better thus and known to be contemn'd,
Than still contemn'd and flatter'd. To be worst,
Than lowest and most dejected thing of
    fortune,
Stands still in esperance, lives not in fear.
5 The lamentable change is from the best;
The worst returns to laughter. Welcome, then,
Thou unsubstantial air that I embrace!
The wretch that thou hast blown unto the worst
Owes nothing to thy blasts.

[Enter GLOUCESTER led by an OLD MAN.]

                                    But who comes here?
10 My father, poorly led? World, world, O world!
But that thy strange mutations make us hate
    thee,
Life would not yield to age.

Old Man
O my good lord, I have been your tenant, and
your father's tenant, these fourscore years.

Gloucester
15 Away, get thee away; good friend, be gone.
Thy comforts can do me no good at all;
Thee they may hurt.

Old Man
You cannot see your way.

Gloucester
I have no way, and therefore want no eyes;
20 I stumbled when I saw: full oft 'tis seen

Our means secure us, and our mere defects
Prove our commodities. O dear son Edgar,
The food of thy abused father's wrath!
Might I but live to see thee in my touch,
I'd say I had eyes again!

Old Man

How now! Who's there?   25

Edgar

[Aside] O gods! Who is't can say 'I am at the
  worst'?
I am worse than e'er I was.

Old Man

'Tis poor mad Tom.

Edgar

[Aside] And worse I may be yet. The worst is
  not
So long as we can say 'This is the worst'.

Old Man

Fellow, where goest?

Gloucester

                              Is it a beggar-man? 30

Old Man

Madman and beggar too.

Gloucester

He has some reason, else he could not beg.
I' th' last night's storm I such a fellow saw;
Which made me think a man a worm. My son
Came then into my mind; and yet my mind   35
Was then scarce friends with him. I have heard
  more since.
As flies to wanton boys are we to th' gods –
They kill us for their sport.

Edgar

[Aside]   How should this be?
Bad is the trade that must play fool to sorrow,
Ang'ring itself and others. – Bless thee, master! 40

Gloucester

Is that the naked fellow?

Old man

Ay, my lord.

Gloucester

Then, prithee, get thee away. If for my sake
Thou wilt o'ertake us hence a mile or twain
I' th' way toward Dover, do it for ancient love;
45   And bring some covering for this naked soul,
Which I'll entreat to lead me.

Old man

Alack, sir, he is mad.

Gloucester

'Tis the times' plague when madmen lead the
blind.
Do as I bid thee, or rather do thy pleasure;
Above the rest, be gone.

Old Man

50   I'll bring him the best 'parel that I have, Come
on't what will.

[Exit.]

Gloucester

Sirrah, naked fellow!

Edgar

Poor Tom's a-cold. *[Aside]* I cannot daub it
further.

Gloucester

Come hither, fellow.

Edgar

[Aside] And yet I must.– Bless thy sweet eyes,
55   they bleed.

Gloucester

Know'st thou the way to Dover?

Edgar

Both stile and gate, horse-way and footpath. Poor
Tom hath been scar'd out of his good wits. Bless
thee, good man's son, from the foul fiend! Five
fiends have been in poor Tom at once: of lust, as
Obidicut; Hobbididence, prince of dumbness;

Mahu, of stealing; Modo, of murder; Flibertigibbet, of mopping and mowing, who since possesses chambermaids and waiting-women. So, bless thee, master!

Gloucester

Here, take this purse, thou whom the heavens'
  plagues   65
Have humbled to all strokes. That I am
  wretched
Makes thee the happier. Heavens, deal so still!
Let the superfluous and lust-dieted man
That slaves your ordinance, that will not see
Because he does not feel, feel your power
  quickly;   70
So distribution should undo excess,
And each man have enough. Dost thou know
  Dover?

Edgar

Ay, master.

Gloucester

There is a cliff whose high and bending head
Looks fearfully in the confined deep: 75
Bring me but to the very brim of it
And I'll repair the misery thou dost bear
With something rich about me. From that place
I shall no leading need.

Edgar

                      Give me thy arm;
Poor Tom shall lead thee.

                    [Exeunt.]

Scene II.

Before the Duke of Albany's palace.

[Enter GONERIL and EDMUND.]

Goneril
    Welcome, my lord. I marvel our mild husband
    Not met us on the way.

[Enter OSWALD.]

                    Now, where's your master?

Oswald
    Madam, within, but never man so chang'd.
    I told him of the army that was landed;
5   He smil'd at it. I told him you were coming;
    His answer was 'The worse'. Of Gloucester's treachery,
    And of the loyal service of his son,
    When I inform'd him, then he call'd me sot,
    And told me I had turn'd the wrong side out.
    What most he should dislike seems pleasant to
10   him;
    What like, offensive.

Goneril
    [To EDMUND] Then shall you go no further.
    It is the cowish terror of his spirit
    That dares not undertake; he'll not feel wrongs
    Which tie him to an answer. Our wishes on the
      way.
15   May prove effects. Back, Edmund, to my brother;
    Hasten his musters and conduct his pow'rs.
    I must change arms at home, and give the
      distaff
    Into my husband's hands. This trusty servant
    Shall pass between us. Ere long you are like to
      hear,
20   If you dare venture in your own behalf,
    A mistress's command. Wear this; spare speech.

[Giving a favour.]

Decline your head; this kiss, if it durst speak,
Would stretch thy spirits up into the air.
Conceive, and fare thee well.

Edmund

Yours in the ranks of death.

Goneril

My most dear Gloucester. 25

[Exit EDMUND.]

O, the difference of man and man!
To thee a woman's services are due.
My fool usurps my body.

Oswald

Madam, here comes my lord.

[Exit.]

[Enter ALBANY.]

Goneril

I have been worth the whistle.

Albany

O Goneril!
You are not worth the dust which the rude wind 30
Blows in your face. I fear your disposition:
That nature which contemns it origin
Cannot be border'd certain in itself;
She that herself will sliver and disbranch
From her material sap perforce must wither 35
And come to deadly use.

Goneril

No more; the text is foolish.

Albany

Wisdom and goodness to the vile seem vile;
Filths savour but themselves. What have you
done?
Tigers, not daughters, what have you
perform'd?

40

109

A father, and a gracious aged man,
Whose reverence even the head-lugg'd bear
   would lick,
Most barbarous, most degenerate, have you
   madded.
Could my good brother suffer you to do it?
45   A man, a Prince, by him so benefited!
If that the heavens do not their visible spirits
Send quickly down to tame these vile offences,
It will come
Humanity must perforce prey on itself,
Like monsters of the deep.

Goneril

50   Milk-liver'd man!
That bear'st a cheek for blows, a head for
   wrongs;
Who hast not in thy brows an eye discerning
Thine honour from thy suffering; that not
   know'st
Fools do those villains pity who are punish'd
Ere they have done their mischief. Where's thy
55   drum?
France spreads his banners in our noiseless
   land,
With plumed helm thy state begins to threat,
Whil'st thou, a moral fool, sits still, and cries
'Alack, why does he so?'

Albany

                    See thyself, devil!
60   Proper deformity shows not in the fiend
So horrid as in woman.

Goneril

              O vain fool!

Albany

Thou changed and self-cover'd thing, for
   shame!
Be-monster not thy feature. Were't my fitness
To let these hands obey my blood,

They are apt enough to dislocate and tear 65
Thy flesh and bones. Howe'er thou art a fiend,
A woman's shape doth shield thee.

Goneril

Marry, your manhood – mew!

[Enter a MESSENGER.]

Albany

What news?

Messenger

O, my good lord, the Duke of Cornwall's dead, 70
Slain by his servant, going to put out
The other eye of Gloucester.

Albany

Gloucester's eyes!

Messenger

A servant that he bred, thrill'd with remorse,
Oppos'd against the act, bending his sword
To his great master; who, thereat enrag'd, 75
Flew on him, and amongst them fell'd him dead;
But not without that harmful stroke which
since
Hath pluck'd him after.

Albany

This shows you are above,
You justicers, that these our nether crimes
So speedily can venge! But, O poor Gloucester! 80
Lost he his other eye?

Messenger

Both, both, my lord.
This letter, madam, craves a speedy answer;
'Tis from your sister.

Goneril

[Aside] One way I like this well;
But being widow, and my Gloucester with her,
May all the building in my fancy pluck 85
Upon my hateful life. Another way
The news is not so tart. – I'll read, and answer.

[Exit.]

Albany
Where was his son, when they did take his eyes?
Messenger
Come with my lady hither.
Albany
He is not here.

Messenger
90   No, my good lord; I met him back again.
Albany
Knows he the wickedness?
Messenger
Ay, my good lord; 'twas he inform'd against
      him
And quit the house on purpose that their
      punishment
Might have the freer course.
Albany
Gloucester, I live
To thank thee for the love thou show'dst the
95   King,
And to revenge thine eyes. Come hither, friend:
Tell me what more thou know'st.

[Exeunt.]

Scene III.

The French camp near Dover.

[Enter KENT *and a* GENTLEMAN.*]*

Kent

Why the King of France is so suddenly gone back
know you no reason?

Gentleman

Something he left imperfect in the state, which
since his coming forth is thought of, which imports
to the kingdom so much fear and danger that his
personal return was most required and necessary.   6

Kent

Who hath he left behind him general?

Gentleman

The Marshal of France, Monsieur La Far.

Kent

Did your letters pierce the Queen to any demon-
stration of grief?   10

Gentleman

Ay, sir; she took them, read them in my
  presence,
And now and then an ample tear trill'd down
Her delicate cheek. It seem'd she was a queen
Over her passion, who, most rebel-like,
Sought to be king o'er her.

Kent

                      O, then it mov'd her.   15

Gentleman

Not to a rage; patience and sorrow strove
Who should express her goodliest. You have
  seen
Sunshine and rain at once: her smiles and tears
Were like a better way. Those happy smilets
That play'd on her ripe lip seem'd not to know   20
What guests were in her eyes, which parted
  thence

113

As pearls from diamonds dropp'd. In brief,
Sorrow would be a rarity most beloved
If all could so become it.

Kent

Made she no verbal question?

Gentleman

25 Faith, once or twice she heav'd the name of
    father
    Pantingly forth, as if it press'd her heart;
    Cried 'Sisters! sisters! Shame of ladies! Sisters!
    Kent! father! sisters! What i' th' storm? i' th'
    night?
    Let pity not be believ'd!' There she shook

30 The holy water from her heavenly eyes,
    And clamour moisten'd; then away she started
    To deal with grief alone.

Kent

It is the stars,
The stars above us, govern our conditions,
Else one self mate and make could not beget
Such different issues. You spoke not with her

35 since?

Gentleman

No.

Kent

Was this before the King return'd?

Gentleman

No, since.

Kent

Well, sir, the poor distressed Lear's i' th' town;
Who sometime in his better tune remembers

40 What we are come about, and by no means
    Will yield to see his daughters.

Gentleman

Why, good sir?

Kent

A sovereign shame so elbows him; his own
unkindness,

114

That stripp'd her from his benediction, turn'd
   her
To foreign casualties, gave her dear rights
To his dog-hearted daughters – these things
   sting   45
His mind so venomously that burning shame
Detains him from Cordelia.
Gentleman
                         Alack, poor gentleman!
Kent
   Of Albany's and Cornwall's powers you heard
      not?
Gentleman
   'Tis so; they are afoot.
Kent
   Well, sir, I'll bring you to our master Lear,   50
   And leave you to attend him. Some dear cause
   Will in concealment wrap me up awhile;
   When I am known aright, you shall not grieve
   Lending me this acquaintance. I pray you go
   Along with me.   55

                    [Exeunt.]

Scene IV.

The French camp. A tent.

[Enter with drum and colours, CORDELIA, DOCTOR, and SOLDIERS.]

Cordelia

Alack, 'tis he! Why, he was met even now
As mad as the vex'd sea, singing aloud,
Crown'd with rank fumiter and furrow weeds,
With hardocks, hemlock, nettles, cuckoo-flow'rs,
5   Darnel, and all the idle weeds that grow
In our sustaining corn. A century send forth;
Search every acre in the high-grown field,
And bring him to our eye.

[Exit an OFFICER.]

What can man's wisdom,
In the restoring his bereaved sense?
10   He that helps him, take all my outward worth.

Doctor

There is means, madam.
Our foster-nurse of nature is repose,
The which he lacks; that to provoke in him
Are many simples operative, whose power
Will close the eye of anguish.

Cordelia

All blest secrets,
15   All you unpublish'd virtues of the earth,
Spring with my tears; be aidant and remediate,
In the good man's distress. Seek, seek for him;
Lest his ungovern'd rage dissolve the life
That wants the means to lead it.

[Enter a MESSENGER.]

Messenger

20   News, madam:
The British pow'rs are marching hitherward.

Cordelia
'Tis known before; our preparation stands
In expectation of them. O dear father!
It is thy business that I go about;
Therefore great France   25
My mourning and importun'd tears hath pitied.
No blown ambition doth our arms incite,
But love, dear love, and our ag'd father's right.
Soon may I hear and see him!

[Exeunt.]

Scene V

Gloucester's castle.

[Enter REGAN and OSWALD.]

Regan
But are my brother's pow'rs set forth?
Oswald
                              Ay madam.

Regan
Himself in person there?
Oswald
                              Madam, with much ado.
Your sister is the better soldier.

Regan
Lord Edmund spake not with your lord at home?
Oswald
5   No, madam.
Regan
What might import my sister's letter to him?
Oswald
I know not, lady.
Regan
Faith, he is posted hence on serious matter.
It was great ignorance, Gloucester's eyes being
       out,
10   To let him live; where he arrives he moves
All hearts against us. Edmund, I think, is gone
In pity of his misery, to dispatch
His nighted life; moreover, to descry
The strength o' th' enemy.
Oswald
15   I must needs after him, madam, with my letter.
Regan
Our troops set forth to-morrow: stay with us;
The ways are dangerous.
Oswald
                              I may not, madam:

My lady charg'd my duty in this business.

Regan

Why should she write to Edmund? Might not you

Transport her purposes by word? Belike   20

Some things – I know not what. I'll love thee much –

Let me unseal the letter.

Oswald

Madam, I had rather –

Regan

I know your lady does not love her husband;

I am sure of that; and at her late being here

She gave strange oeillades and most speaking looks

To noble Edmund. I know you are of her   25
bosom.

Oswald

I, madam?

Regan

I speak in understanding; y'are, I know't.

Therefore I do advise you take this note.

My lord is dead; Edmund and I have talk'd;   30

And more convenient is he for my hand

Than for your lady's. You may gather more.

If you do find him, pray you give him this;

And when your mistress hears thus much from you,

I pray desire her call her wisdom to her.   35

So fare you well.

If you do chance to hear of that blind traitor,

Preferment falls on him that cuts him off.

Oswald

Would I could meet him, madam! I should show

What party I do follow.

Regan

Fare thee well.   40

[Exeunt.]

Scene VI.

The country near Dover.

[Enter GLOUCESTER, and EDGAR dressed like a peasant.]

Gloucester
When shall I come to th' top of that same hill?

Edgar
You do climb up it now; look how we labour.

Gloucester
Methinks the ground is even.

Edgar
Horrible steep.

Hark, do you hear the sea?

Gloucester
No, truly.

Edgar
5   Why then, your other senses grow imperfect
By your eyes' anguish.

Gloucester
So may it be indeed.

Methinks thy voice is alter'd, and thou speak'st
In better phrase and matter than thou didst.

Edgar
Y'are much deceiv'd: in nothing am I chang'd
But in my garments.

Gloucester
10   Methinks y'are better spoken.

Edgar
Come on, sir; here's the place. Stand still. How fearful
And dizzy 'tis to cast one's eyes so low!
The crows and choughs that wing the mid-way air
Show scarce so gross as beetles. Half-way down
Hangs one that gathers samphire – dreadful
15   trade!
Methinks he seems no bigger than his head.

The fishermen that walk upon the beach
Appear like mice; and yond tall anchoring bark
Diminish'd to her cock; her cock, a buoy
Almost too small for sight. The murmuring
    surge   20
That on th' unnumb'red idle pebble chafes
Cannot be heard so high. I'll look no more;
Lest my brain turn, and the deficient sight
Topple down headlong.

Gloucester
                                        Set me where you stand.
Edgar
Give me your hand. You are now within a foot   25
Of th' extreme verge. For all beneath the moon
Would I not leap upright.

Gloucester
                                        Let go my hand.
Here, friend, 's another purse; in it a jewel
Well worth a poor man's taking. Fairies and
    gods
Prosper it with thee! Go thou further off;   30
Bid me farewell, and let me hear thee going.

Edgar
Now fare ye well, good sir.

Gloucester
                                        With all my heart.

Edgar
Why I do trifle thus with his despair
Is done to cure it.

Gloucester
[Kneeling] O you mighty gods!
This world I do renounce, and in your sights   35
Shake patiently my great affliction off.
If I could bear it longer, and not fall
To quarrel with your great opposeless wills,
My snuff and loathed part of nature should
Burn itself out. If Edgar live, O, bless him!   40
[Rising] Now, fellow, fare thee well.

Edgar

Gone, sir; farewell,

[GLOUCESTER casts himself down.]

And yet I know not how conceit may rob
The treasury of life, when life itself
Yields to the theft. Had he been where he
    thought,
By this had thought been past. – Alive or
45   dead?
Ho, you sir! friend! Hear you, sir! Speak! –
Thus might he pass indeed. Yet he revives –
What are you, sir?

Gloucester

Away, and let me die.

Edgar

Hadst thou been aught but gossamer, feathers,
    air,
50 So many fathom down precipitating,
Thou'dst shiver'd like an egg; but thou dost
    breathe,
Hast heavy substance, bleed'st not, speak'st, art
    sound.
Ten masts at each make not the altitude
Which thou hast perpendicularly fell.
55 Thy life's a miracle. Speak yet again.

Gloucester

But have I fall'n, or no?

Edgar

From the dread summit of this chalky bourn.
Look up a-height; the shrill-gorg'd lark so far
Cannot be seen or heard. Do but look up.

Gloucester

60 Alack, I have no eyes.
Is wretchedness depriv'd that benefit,
To end itself by death? 'Twas yet some comfort,
When misery could beguile the tyrant's rage
And frustrate his proud will.

Edgar

                  Give me your arm.
Up – so. How is't? Feel you your legs? You stand. 65

Gloucester

  Too well, too well.

Edgar

              This is above all strangeness.
Upon the crown o' th' cliff what thing was that
Which parted from you?

Gloucester

              A poor unfortunate beggar.

Edgar

  As I stood here below, methought his eyes
Were two full moons; he had a thousand noses, 70
Horns whelk'd and waved like the enridged sea.
It was some fiend; therefore, thou happy father,
Think that the clearest gods, who make them
    honours
Of men's impossibilities, have preserved thee.

Gloucester

  I do remember now. Henceforth I'll bear 75
Affliction till it do cry out itself
'Enough, enough' and die. That thing you
    speak of
I took it for a man; often 'twould say,
'The fiend, the fiend'. He led me to that place.

Edgar

  Bear free and patient thoughts.

    [Enter LEAR, *fantastically dressed with weeds.]*

                  But who comes here? 80
The safer sense will ne'er accommodate
His master thus.

Lear

  No, they cannot touch me for coining: I am
    the King himself.

Edgar

  O thou side-piercing sight! 85

Lear

Nature's above art in that respect.
There's your press-money. That fellow handles his
bow like a crow-keeper; draw me a clothier's yard.
Look, look, a mouse! Peace, peace: this piece of
toasted cheese will do't. There's my gauntlet; I'll
prove it on a giant. Bring up the brown bills. O,
well flown, bird! i' the clout, i' the clout – hewgh!

92   Give the word.

Edgar

Sweet marjoram.

Lear

Pass.

Gloucester

95   I know that voice.

Lear

Ha! Goneril, with a white beard! They flatter'd
me like a dog, and told me I had white hairs in
my beard ere the black ones were there. To say
'ay' and 'no' to everything that I said! 'Ay' and
'no' too was no good divinity. When the rain
came to wet me once, and the wind to make me
chatter; when the thunder would not peace at
my bidding; there I found 'em, there I smelt 'em
out. Go to, they are not men o' their words. They
told me I was everything; 'tis a lie – I am not

105   ague-proof.

Gloucester

The trick of that voice I do well remember.
Is't not the King?

Lear

Ay, every inch a king.
When I do stare, see how the subject quakes.
I pardon that man's life. What was thy cause?

110   Adultery?
Thou shalt not die. Die for adultery? No.
The wren goes to't, and the small gilded fly
Does lecher in my sight.

Let copulation thrive; for Gloucester's bastard son
Was kinder to his father than my daughters   115
Got 'tween the lawful sheets.
To't, luxury, pell-mell, for I lack soldiers.
Behold yond simp'ring dame
Whose face between her forks presages snow,
That minces virtue and does shake the head   120
To hear of pleasure's name –
The fitchew nor the soiled horse goes to't
With a more riotous appetite.
Down from the waist they are centaurs,
Though women all above;   125
But to the girdle do the gods inherit,
Beneath is all the fiends';
There's hell, there's darkness, there is the
     sulphurous pit –
Burning, scalding, stench, consumption.
Fie, fie, fie! pah, pah! Give me an ounce of civet,
     good apothecary, to sweeten my imagination.
There's money for thee.   131

Gloucester
O, let me kiss that hand!

Lear
Let me wipe it first; it smells of mortality.

Gloucester
O ruin'd piece of nature! This great world
Shall so wear out to nought. Dost thou know
     me?   135

Lear
I remember thine eyes well enough. Dost thou
squiny at me? No, do thy worst, blind Cupid; I'll
not love. Read thou this challenge; mark but the
penning of it.

Gloucester
Were all thy letters suns, I could not see one.   140

Edgar
[*Aside*] I would not take this from report. It is.
And my heart breaks at it.

Lear
Read.

Gloucester
What, with the case of eyes?

Lear

145 O, ho, are you there with me? No eyes in your
head nor no money in your purse? Your eyes are
in a heavy case, your purse in a light; yet you see
how this world goes.

Gloucester

149 I see it feelingly.

Lear
What, art mad? A man may see how this world
goes with no eyes. Look with thine ears. See how
yond justice rails upon yond simple thief. Hark,
in thine ear: change places and, handy-dandy,
which is the justice, which is the thief? Thou hast

155 seen a farmer's dog bark at a beggar?

Gloucester
Ay, sir.

Lear
And the creature run from the cur?
There thou mightst behold the great image of
authority: a dog's obey'd in office.

160 Thou rascal beadle, hold thy bloody hand.
Why dost thou lash that whore? Strip thy own
back;
Thou hotly lusts to use her in that kind
For which thou whip'st her. The usurer hangs
the cozener.
Through tatter'd clothes small vices do appear;
Robes and furr'd gowns hide all. Plate sin with

165 gold,
And the strong lance of justice hurtless breaks;
Arm it in rags, a pigmy's straw does pierce it.
None does offend, none – I say none; I'll able
'em.
Take that of me, my friend, who have the power

To seal th' accuser's lips. Get thee glass eyes,   170
And, like a scurvy politician, seem
To see the things thou dost not. Now, now,
   now, now!
Pull off my boots. Harder, harder – so.

Edgar

O, matter and impertinency mix'd!
Reason in madness!   176

Lear

If thou wilt weep my fortunes, take my eyes.
I know thee well enough; thy name is
   Gloucester.
Thou must be patient; we came crying hither.
Thou know'st the first time that we smell the
   air   180
We wawl and cry. I will preach to thee. Mark.

Gloucester

Alack, alack the day!

Lear

When we are born, we cry that we are come
To this great stage of fools. This is a good
   block!
It were a delicate stratagem to shoe   185
A troop of horse with felt; I'll put't in proof;
And when I have stol'n upon these son-in-laws,
Then kill, kill, kill, kill, kill, kill!

[Enter a GENTLEMAN, *with* ATTENDANTS.*]*

Gentleman

O, here he is: lay hand upon him – Sir,
Your most dear daughter –   190

Lear

No rescue? What, a prisoner? I am even
The natural fool of fortune. Use me well;
You shall have ransom. Let me have surgeons;
I am cut to th' brains.

Gentleman

          You shall have any thing.

Lear
No seconds? All myself?
Why, this would make a man a man of salt,
To use his eyes for garden water-pots,
Ay, and laying Autumn's dust.

Gentleman
                                                    Good sir –

Lear
I will die bravely, like a smug bridegroom.

200 What!
I will be jovial. Come, come; I am a king,
My masters, know you that.

Gentleman
You are a royal one, and we obey you.

Lear
Then there's life in't. Nay, an you get it, you shall
get it by running. Sa, sa, sa, sa.

[Exit running; ATTENDANTS *follow.]*

Gentleman
206 A sight most pitiful in the meanest wretch,
Past speaking of in a king! Thou hast one
      daughter
Who redeems nature from the general curse
Which twain have brought her to.

Edgar
Hail, gentle sir.

Gentleman
Sir, speed you; what's your will?

Edgar
211 Do you hear aught, sir, of a battle toward?

Gentleman
Most sure and vulgar; every one hears that
Which can distinguish sound.

Edgar
                                                    But, by your favour,
How near's the other army?

Gentleman
    Near and on speedy foot; the main descry   215
    Stands on the hourly thought.
Edgar
                         I thank you, sir; that's all.
Gentleman
    Though that the Queen on special cause is here.
    Her army is mov'd on.
Edgar
                            I thank you, sir.

[Exit GENTLEMAN.]

Gloucester
    You ever-gentle gods, take my breath from me;
    Let not my worser spirit tempt me again   220
    To die before you please.
Edgar
                    Well pray you, father.
Gloucester
    Now, good sir, what are you?
Edgar
    A most poor man, made tame to fortune's
        blows,
    Who, by the art of known and feeling sorrows,
    Am pregnant to good pity. Give me your hand;   225
    I'll lead you to some biding.
Gloucester
                    Hearty thanks;
    The bounty and the benison of heaven
    To boot, and boot!

[Enter OSWALD.]

Oswald
    A proclaim'd prize! Most happy!
    That eyeless head of thine was first fram'd flesh
    To raise my fortunes. Thou old unhappy traitor,   230
    Briefly thyself remember. The sword is out
    That must destroy thee.

Gloucester
                              Now let thy friendly hand
Put strength enough to't.

[EDGAR *interposes.*]

Oswald
                              Wherefore, bold peasant,
Dar'st thou support a publish'd traitor? Hence;
235   Lest that th' infection of his fortune take
Like hold on thee. Let go his arm.

Edgar
Chill not let go, zir, without vurther 'casion.

Oswald
Let go, slave, or thou diest.

Edgar
Good gentleman, go your gait, and let poor volk
pass. An chud ha' bin zwagger'd out of my life,
'twould not ha' bin zo long as 'tis by a vortnight.
Nay, come not near th' old man; keep out, che
vor ye, or Ice try whether your costard or my
ballow be the harder. Chill be plain with you.

Oswald
245   Out, dunghill!

Edgar
Chill pick your teeth, zir. Come; no matter vor
your foins.

[*They fight.*]

Oswald
Slave, thou hast slain me. Villain, take my
purse;
If ever thou wilt thrive, bury my body,
And give the letters which thou find'st about
250   me
To Edmund Earl of Gloucester. Seek him out
Upon the English party. O, untimely death!
Death!

[*He dies.*]

Edgar

    I know thee well; a serviceable villain,
    As duteous to the vices of thy mistress   255
    As badness would desire.

Gloucester

                       What, is he dead?

Edgar

    Sit you down, father; rest you.
    Let's see these pockets; the letters that he
      speaks of
    May be my friends. He's dead; I am only sorry
    He had no other death's-man. Let us see.   260
    Leave, gentle wax; and, manners, blame us not:
    To know our enemies' minds we'd rip their
      hearts;
    Their papers is more lawful.
    [Reads] 'Let our reciprocal vows be rememb'red.
    You have many opportunities to cut him off; if
    your will want not, time and place will be fruit-
    fully offer'd. There is nothing done if he return
    the conqueror: then am I the prisoner, and his
    bed my gaol; from the loathed warmth whereof
    deliver me, and supply the place for your labour. 268
    Your (wife, so I would say) affectionate servant,
                         GONERIL.'
    O indistinguish'd space of woman's will!
    A plot upon her virtuous husband's life;
    And the exchange my brother! Here, in the
      sands
    Thee I'll rake up, the post unsanctified
    Of murderous lechers; and in the mature time   275
    With this ungracious paper strike the sight
    Of the death-practis'd duke. For him 'tis well
    That of thy death and business I can tell.

Gloucester

    The King is mad; how stiff is my vile sense,
    That I stand up, and have ingenious feeling   280
    Of my huge sorrows! Better I were distract;

So should my thoughts be sever'd from my
    griefs,
And woes by wrong imaginations lose
The knowledge of themselves.

[Drum afar off.]

Edgar
                                    Give me your hand.
Far off methinks I hear the beaten drum.
Come, father, I'll bestow you with a friend.

[Exeunt.]

Scene VII.

A tent in the French camp.

[Music. Enter CORDELIA, KENT, DOCTOR, *and* GENTLEMAN.*]*

Cordelia

O thou good Kent, how shall I live and work
To match thy goodness? My life will be too
    short,
And every measure fail me.

Kent

To be acknowledg'd, madam, is o'erpaid.
All my reports go with the modest truth;   5
Nor more nor clipp'd, but so.

Cordelia

                    Be better suited.
These weeds are memories of those worser
    hours;
I prithee put them off.

Kent

                    Pardon, dear madam;
Yet to be known shortens my made intent:
My boon I make it that you know me not   10
Till time and I think meet.

Cordelia

Then be't so, my good lord. *[To the* DOCTOR*]* How
does the King?

Doctor

Madam, sleeps still.

Cordelia

O you kind gods,
Cure this great breach in his abused nature!
Th' untun'd and jarring senses, O, wind up   15
Of this child-changed father!

Doctor

                    So please your Majesty
That we may wake the King; he hath slept
    long.

133

Cordelia
>Be govern'd by your knowledge, and proceed
>I' th' sway of your own will. *[To the* GENTLEMAN*]*
20   Is he array'd?

Gentleman
>Ay, madam; in the heaviness of sleep
>We put fresh garments on him.

Doctor
>Be by, good madam, when we do awake him;
>I doubt not of his temperance.

Cordelia
>   Very well.

Doctor
25   Please you, draw near. Louder the music there!

[He draws the curtains and discovers LEAR *asleep in bed.]*

Cordelia
>O my dear father! Restoration hang
>Thy medicine on my lips, and let this kiss
>Repair those violent harms that my two sisters
>Have in thy reverence made.

Kent
>   Kind and dear princess!

Cordelia
>Had you not been their father, these white
30   flakes
>Did challenge pity of them. Was this a face
>To be oppos'd against the warring winds?
>To stand against the deep dread bolted
>   thunder?
>In the most terrible and nimble stroke
>Of quick cross lightning? to watch – poor
35   perdu! –
>With this thin helm? Mine enemy's dog,
>Though he had bit me, should have stood that
>   night
>Against my fire; and wast thou fain, poor
>   father,

To hovel thee with swine and rogues forlorn,
In short and musty straw? Alack, alack!   40
'Tis wonder that thy life and wits at once
Had not concluded all. – He wakes; speak to
   him.

Doctor

Madam, do you; 'tis fittest.

Cordelia

How does my royal lord? How fares your
   Majesty?

Lear

You do me wrong to take me out o' th' grave.   45
Thou art a soul in bliss; but I am bound
Upon a wheel of fire, that mine own tears
Do scald like molten lead.

Cordelia

                                          Sir, do you know me?

Lear

You are a spirit, I know. Where did you die?

Cordelia

Still, still far wide!   50

Doctor

He's scarce awake; let him alone awhile.

Lear

Where have I been? Where am I? Fair daylight?
I am mightily abus'd. I should e'en die with
   pity
To see another thus. I know not what to say.
I will not swear these are my hands. Let's see.   55
I feel this pin prick. Would I were assur'd
Of my condition!

Cordelia

                              O, look upon me, sir,
And hold your hands in benediction o'er me.
No, sir, you must not kneel.

Lear

                                          Pray, do not mock me:
I am a very foolish fond old man,   60

Fourscore and upward, not an hour more nor
less;
And, to deal plainly,
I fear I am not in my perfect mind.
Methinks I should know you, and know this
man;
65   Yet I am doubtful; for I am mainly ignorant
What place this is; and all the skill I have
Remembers not these garments; nor I know
not
Where I did lodge last night. Do not laugh at
me;
For, as I am a man, I think this lady
To be my child Cordelia.

Cordelia

70   And so I am, I am.

Lear

Be your tears wet? Yes, faith. I pray weep not;
If you have poison for me I will drink it.
I know you do not love me; for your sisters
Have, as I do remember, done me wrong:
You have some cause, they have not.

Cordelia

75   No cause, no cause.

Lear

Am I in France?

Kent

                 In your own kingdom, sir.

Lear

Do not abuse me.

Doctor

Be comforted, good madam. The great rage,
You see, is kill'd in him; and yet it is danger
80   To make him even o'er the time he has lost.
Desire him to go in; trouble him no more
Till further settling.

Cordelia

Will't please your Highness walk?

Lear
>   You must bear with me.
> Pray you now, forget and forgive; I am old and
>   foolish.   85

>   *[Exeunt all but* KENT *and* GENTLEMAN.*]*

Gentleman
>   Holds it true, sir, that the Duke of Cornwall was
>   so slain?

Kent
>   Most certain, sir.

Gentleman
>   Who is conductor of his people?

Kent
>   As 'tis said, the bastard son of Gloucester.   90

Gentleman
>   They say Edgar, his banish'd son, is with the Earl
>   of Kent in Germany.

Kent
>   Report is changeable. 'Tis time to look about; the
>   powers of the kingdom approach apace.

Gentleman
>   The arbitrement is like to be bloody. Fare you
>   well, sir.

>   *[Exit.]*

Kent
>   My point and period will be throughly
>   wrought,   97
>   Or well or ill, as this day's battle's fought.

>   *[Exit.]*

ACT FIVE
Scene I

The British camp near Dover.

[Enter, with drum and colours, EDMUND, REGAN, GENTLEMEN, and SOLDIERS.]

Edmund
 Know of the Duke if his last purpose hold,
 Or whether since he is advis'd by aught
 To change the course. He's full of alteration
 And self-reproving – bring his constant
     pleasure.

[Exit an OFFICER.]

Regan
5 Our sister's man is certainly miscarried.
Edmund
 'Tis to be doubted, madam
Regan
                    Now, sweet lord,
 You know the goodness I intend upon you.
 Tell me – but truly – but then speak the truth –
 Do you not love my sister?
Edmund
                    In honour'd love.
Regan
10 But have you never found my brother's way
 To the forfended place?
Edmund
                    That thought abuses you.
Regan
 I am doubtful that you have been conjunct
 And bosom'd with her, as far as we call hers.
Edmund
 No, by mine honour, madam.

138

Regan
    I never shall endure her. Dear my lord,   15
    Be not familiar with her.

Edmund
                Fear me not.
    She and the Duke her husband!

[Enter, with drum and colours, ALBANY, GONERIL, *and*
                SOLDIERS.*]*

Goneril
    [Aside] I had rather lose the battle than that
        sister
    Should loosen him and me.

Albany
    Our very loving sister, well be-met.   20
    Sir, this I heard: the King is come to his
        daughter
    With others whom the rigour of our state
    Forc'd to cry out. Where I could not be honest
    I never yet was valiant. For this business,
    It touches us as France invades our land,   25
    Not bolds the King, with others whom, I fear.
    Most just and heavy causes make oppose.

Edmund
    Sir, you speak nobly.

Regan
              Why is this reason'd?

Goneril
    Combine together 'gainst the enemy;
    For these domestic-door particulars   30
    Are not the question here.

Albany
              Let's then determine
    With th' ancient of war on our proceeding.

Edmund
    I shall attend you presently at your tent.

Regan
    Sister, you'll go with us?

Goneril

35   No.

Regan

    'Tis most convenient; pray you go with us.

Goneril

    [Aside] O, ho, I know the riddle. – I will go.

[As they are going out, enter EDGAR, *disguised.]*

Edgar

    If e'er your Grace had speech with man so poor
    Hear me one word.

Albany

                    I'll overtake you. – Speak.

[Exeunt all but ALBANY *and* EDGAR.*]*

Edgar

40   Before you fight the battle, ope this letter.
    If you have victory, let the trumpet sound
    For him that brought it; wretched though I
        seem
    I can produce a champion that will prove
    What is avouched there. If you miscarry,
45   Your business of the world hath so an end,
    And machination ceases. Fortune love you!

Albany

    Stay till I have read the letter.

Edgar

                    I was forbid it.
    When time shall serve, let but the herald cry,
    And I'll appear again.

Albany

50   Why, fare thee well. I will o'erlook thy paper.

[Exit EDGAR.*]*

[Re-enter EDMUND.*]*

Edmund

    The enemy's in view; draw up your powers.

Here is the guess of their true strength and
    forces
By diligent discovery; but your haste
Is now urg'd on you.

Albany

                We will greet the time.

        [Exit.]

Edmund

To both these sisters have I sworn my love;   55
Each jealous of the other, as the stung
Are of the adder. Which of them shall I take?
Both? one? or neither? Neither can be enjoy'd,
If both remain alive: to take the widow,
Exasperates, makes mad her sister Goneril;   60
And hardly shall I carry out my side,
Her husband being alive. Now then, we'll use
His countenance for the battle; which being
    done,
Let her who would be rid of him devise
His speedy taking off. As for the mercy   65
Which he intends to Lear and to Cordelia –
The battle done, and they within our power,
Shall never see his pardon; for my state
Stands on me to defend, not to debate.

        [Exit.]

Scene II.

A field between the two camps.

[Alarum within. Enter, with drum and colours, the Powers of France over the stage, CORDELIA with her Father in her hand, and exeunt.]

[Enter EDGAR and GLOUCESTER.]

Edgar

Here, father, take the shadow of this tree
For your good host; pray that the right may
   thrive.
If ever I return to you again
I'll bring you comfort.

Gloucester

Grace go with you, sir!

[Exit EDGAR.]

[Alarum and retreat within. Re-enter EDGAR.]

Edgar

5   Away, old man; give me thy hand; away!
King Lear hath lost, he and his daughter ta'en.
Give me thy hand; come on.

Gloucester

No further, sir; a man may rot even here.

Edgar

What, in ill thoughts again? Men must endure
10   Their going hence, even as their coming hither:
Ripeness is all. Come on.

Gloucester

And that's true too.

[Exeunt.]

Scene III.

The British camp near Dover.

[Enter, in conquest, with drum and colours, EDMUND; LEAR and CORDELIA prisoners; SOLDIERS, CAPTAIN.]

Edmund
Some officers take them away. Good guard,
Until their greater pleasures first be known
That are to censure them.

Cordelia
                We are not the first
Who with best meaning have incurr'd the worst.
For thee, oppressed King, am I cast down;   5
Myself could else out-frown false Fortune's frown.
Shall we not see these daughters and these sisters?

Lear
No, no, no, no! Come, let's away to prison.
We two alone will sing like birds i' th' cage;
When thou dost ask me blessing, I'll kneel down   10
And ask of thee forgiveness; so we'll live,
And pray, and sing, and tell old tales, and laugh
At gilded butterflies, and hear poor rogues
Talk of court news; and we'll talk with them too –
Who loses and who wins; who's in, who's out –   15
And take upon's the mystery of things
As if we were God's spies; and we'll wear out
In a wall'd prison packs and sects of great ones
That ebb and flow by th' moon.

Edmund
                Take them away.

Lear

20   Upon such sacrifices, my Cordelia,
The gods themselves throw incense. Have I
    caught thee?
He that parts us shall bring a brand from
    heaven
And fire us hence like foxes. Wipe thine eyes;
The good years shall devour them, flesh and
    fell,
Ere they shall make us weep. We'll see 'em
25   starv'd first.
Come.

    [Exeunt LEAR *and* CORDELIA, *guarded.]*

Edmund

Come hither, Captain; hark.
[Giving a paper] Take thou this note; go follow
    them to prison.
One step I have advanc'd thee; if thou dost
30   As this instructs thee, thou dost make thy way
To noble fortunes. Know thou this, that men
Are as the time is; to be tender-minded
Does not become a sword. Thy great
    employment
Will not bear question; either say thou'lt do't,
Or thrive by other means.

Captain

                      I'll do't, my lord.
35 *Edmund*

About it; and write happy when th' hast done.
Mark – I say, instantly; and carry it so
As I have set it down.

Captain

I cannot draw a cart nor eat dried oats;
40   If it be man's work, I'll do't.

    [Exit.]

[Flourish. Enter ALBANY, GONERIL, REGAN, *and* SOLDIERS.]*

Albany

Sir, you have show'd to-day your valiant strain,
And fortune led you well. You have the captives
Who were the opposites of this day's strife;
I do require them of you, so to use them
As we shall find their merits and our safety   45
May equally determine.

Edmund

            Sir, I thought it fit
To send the old and miserable king
To some retention and appointed guard;
Whose age has charms in it, whose title more,
To pluck the common bosom on his side,   50
And turn our impress'd lances in our eyes
Which do command them. With him I sent the
    Queen.
My reason all the same; and they are ready
To-morrow, or at further space, t' appear
Where you shall hold your session. At this
    time   55
We sweat and bleed; the friend hath lost his
    friend;
And the best quarrels, in the heat, are curs'd
By those that feel their sharpness.
The question of Cordelia and her father
Requires a fitter place.

Albany

            Sir, by your patience,   60
I hold you but a subject of this war,
Not as a brother.

Regan

          That's as we list to grace him.
Methinks our pleasure might have been
    demanded
Ere you had spoke so far. He led our powers,
Bore the commission of my place and person,   65
The which immediacy may well stand up
And call itself your brother.

Goneril
                                    Not so hot.
In his own grace he doth exalt himself,
More than in your addition.
Regan
                                    In my rights,
70   By me invested, he compeers the best.
Albany
That were the most, if he should husband you.
Regan
Jesters do oft prove prophets.
Goneril
                                    Holla, holla!
That eye that told you so look'd but asquint.
Regan
Lady, I am not well; else I should answer
75   From a full-flowing stomach. General,
Take thou my soldiers, prisoners, patrimony;
Dispose of them, of me; the walls is thine.
Witness the world that I create thee here
My lord and master.
Goneril
                                    Mean you to enjoy him?
Albany
80   The let-alone lies not in your good will.
Edmund
Nor in thine, lord.
Albany
                                    Half-blooded fellow, yes.
Regan
[*To* EDMUND] Let the drum strike, and prove my
title thine.
Albany
Stay yet; hear reason. Edmund, I arrest thee
On capital treason; and, in thy attaint,

                    [*Pointing to* GONERIL.]

85   This gilded serpent. For your claim, fair sister,

I bar it in the interest of my wife;
'Tis she is sub-contracted to this lord,
And I, her husband, contradict your banns.
If you will marry, make your loves to me –
My lady is bespoke.

Goneril

An interlude!   90

Albany

Thou art arm'd, Gloster. Let the trumpet sound.
If none appear to prove upon thy person
Thy heinous, manifest, and many treasons,
There is my pledge;   *[Throwing down a glove].*
                    I'll make it on thy heart.
Ere I taste bread, thou art in nothing less
Than I have here proclaim'd thee.

Regan

Sick, O, sick!

Goneril

[Aside] If not, I'll ne'er trust medicine.   97

Edmund

There's my exchange. *[Throwing down a glove].*
    What in the world he is
That names me traitor, villain-like he lies.
Call by thy trumpet; he that dares approach.   100
On him, on you, who not, I will maintain
My truth and honour firmly.

Albany

A herald, ho!

Edmund

A herald, ho, a herald!

Albany

Trust to thy single virtue; for thy soldiers,
All levied in my name, have in my name   105
Took their discharge.

Regan

My sickness grows upon me.

Albany

She is not well; convey her to my tent.

[Exit REGAN, led.]

[Enter a HERALD.]

Come hither, herald. Let the trumpet sound,
109 And read out this.

Herald
[Reads] 'If any man of quality or degree within
the lists of the army will maintain upon Edmund,
supposed Earl of Gloucester, that he is a manifold
traitor, let him appear by the third sound of the
114 trumpet. He is bold in his defence.'
Sound, trumpet. *[1 Trumpet.]*

Herald
Again! *[2 Trumpet.]*

Herald
Again! *[3 Trumpet.]*

[Trumpet answers within.]

*[Enter EDGAR, armed, at the third sound, a trumpet before
him.]*

Albany
Ask him his purposes, why he appears Upon this
call o' th' trumpet.

Herald
What are you?
120 Your name, your quality, and why you answer
This present summons?

Edgar
Know, my name is lost,
By treason's tooth bare-gnawn and canker-bit;
Yet am I noble as the adversary
I come to cope.

Albany
Which is that adversary?

Edgar
What's he that speaks for Edmund Earl of
125 Gloucester?

Edmund
　　Himself. What say'st thou to him?
Edgar
　　　　　　　　　Draw thy sword,
　　That, if my speech offend a noble heart,
　　Thy arm may do thee justice; here is mine.
　　Behold, it is the privilege of mine honours,
　　My oath, and my profession. I protest –　　　　130
　　Maugre thy strength, youth, place, and
　　　　eminence,
　　Despite thy victor sword and fire-new fortune,
　　Thy valour and thy heart – thou art a traitor;
　　False to thy gods, thy brother, and thy father;
　　Conspirant 'gainst this high illustrious prince;　135
　　And, from th' extremest upward of thy head
　　To the descent and dust below thy foot.
　　A most toad-spotted traitor. Say thou 'No'.
　　This sword, this arm, and my best spirits, are
　　　　bent
　　To prove upon thy heart, whereto I speak,　　140
　　Thou liest.
Edmund
　　In wisdom I should ask thy name;
　　But, since thy outside looks so fair and warlike,
　　And that thy tongue some say of breeding
　　　　breathes,　　　　　　　　　　　　　143
　　What safe and nicely I might well delay
　　By rule of knighthood, I disdain and spurn.
　　Back do I toss these treasons to thy head;
　　With the hell-hated lie o'erwhelm thy heart;
　　Which – for they yet glance by and scarcely
　　　　bruise –
　　This sword of mine shall give them instant way
　　Where they shall rest for ever. Trumpets, speak.　150

　　　[Alarums. They fight. EDMUND *falls.]*

Albany
　　Save him, save him!

Goneril

                This is practice, Gloucester.
By th' law of war thou wast not bound to
  answer
An unknown opposite; thou art not vanquish'd,
But cozen'd and beguil'd.

Albany

                  Shut your mouth, dame,
155   Or with this paper shall I stopple it. Hold, sir.
Thou worse than any name, read thine own
  evil.
No tearing, lady; I perceive you know it.

Goneril

Say, if I do – the laws are mine, not thine.
Who can arraign me for't?

Albany

               Most monstrous! O!
Know'st thou this paper?

Goneril

160   Ask me not what I know.

[Exit.]

Albany

Go after her. She's desperate; govern her.

[Exit an OFFICER.*]*

Edmund

What you have charg'd me with, that have I
  done,
And more, much more; the time will bring it
  out.
'Tis past, and so am I. But what art thou
165   That hast this fortune on me? If thou'rt noble,
I do forgive thee.

Edgar

            Let's exchange charity.
I am no less in blood than thou art, Edmund;
If more, the more th' hast wrong'd me.

My name is Edgar, and thy father's son.
The gods are just, and of our pleasant vices   170
Make instruments to plague us:
The dark and vicious place where thee he got
Cost him his eyes.

Edmund

            Th' hast spoken right, 'tis true;
The wheel is come full circle; I am here.

Albany

Methought thy very gait did prophesy   175
A royal nobleness. I must embrace thee.
Let sorrow split my heart if ever I
Did hate thee or thy father!

Edgar

            Worthy prince,
I know't.

Albany

            Where have you hid yourself?
How have you known the miseries of your
    father?   180

Edgar

By nursing them, my lord. List a brief tale;
And when 'tis told, O that my heart would
    burst!
The bloody proclamation to escape
That follow'd me so near – O our lives'
    sweetness,
That we the pain of death would hourly die   185
Rather than die at once! – taught me to shift
Into a madman's rags, t' assume a semblance
That very dogs disdain'd; and in this habit
Met I my father with his bleeding rings,
Their precious stones new lost; became his
    guide,   190
Led him, begg'd for him, sav'd him from
    despair;
Never – O fault! – reveal'd myself unto him
Until some half-hour past, when I was arm'd;

195   Not sure, though hoping, of this good success,
I ask'd his blessing, and from first to last
Told him my pilgrimage. But his flaw'd heart –
Alack, too weak the conflict to support! –
'Twixt two extremes of passion, joy and grief,
Burst smilingly.

Edmund
This speech of your hath mov'd me,
And shall perchance do good; but speak you
200   on;
You look as you had something more to say,

Albany
If there be more, more woeful, hold it in;
For I am almost ready to dissolve,
Hearing of this.

Edgar
            This would have seem'd a period
205   To such as love not sorrow; but another,
To amplify too much, would make much more,
And top extremity.
Whilst I was big in clamour, came there in a
    man
Who, having seen me in my worst estate,
210   Shunn'd my abhorr'd society; but then, finding
Who 'twas that so endur'd, with his strong
    arms
He fastened on my neck and bellowed out
As he'd burst heaven; threw him on my father;
Told the most piteous tale of Lear and him
215   That ever ear receiv'd; which in recounting
His grief grew puissant, and the strings of life
Began to crack. Twice then the trumpets
    sounded
And there I left him tranc'd.

Albany
               But who was this?

Edgar
Kent, sir, the banish'd Kent, who in disguise

Follow'd his enemy king, and did him service   220
Improper for a slave.

[Enter a GENTLEMAN *with a bloody knife.]*

Gentleman
Help, help, O, help!

Edgar
                              What kind of help?

Albany
                                        Speak, man.

Edgar
What means this bloody knife?

Gentleman
                              'Tis hot, it smokes;
It came even from the heart of – O, she's dead!

Albany
Who dead? Speak, man.   225

Gentleman
Your lady, sir, your lady! and her sister
By her is poison'd; she confesses it.

Edmund
I was contracted to them both. All three
Now marry in an instant.

Edgar
                              Here comes Kent.

[Enter KENT.*]*

Albany
Produce the bodies, be they alive or dead.   230

[Exit GENTLEMAN.*]*

This judgment of the heavens, that makes us
    tremble,
Touches us not with pity. O, is this he?
The time will not allow the compliment
Which very manners urges.

Kent
                              I am come

153

235   To bid my king and master aye good night.
  Is he not here?

Albany
        Great thing of us forgot!
  Speak, Edmund, where's the King? and where's
   Cordelia?

[The bodies of GONERIL *and* REGAN *are brought in.]*

  See'st thou this object, Kent?

Kent
  Alack, why thus?

Edmund
          Yet Edmund was belov'd.
240   The one the other poison'd for my sake,
  And after slew herself.

Albany
  Even so. Cover their faces.

Edmund
  I pant for life. Some good I mean to do,
  Despite of mine own nature. Quickly send –
245   Be brief in it – to th' castle; for my writ
  Is on the life of Lear and on Cordelia.
  Nay, send in time.

Albany
      Run, run, O, run!

Edgar
  To who, my lord? Who has the office? Send
  Thy token of reprieve.

Edmund
250   Well thought on. Take my sword;
  Give it the Captain.

Albany
       Haste thee, for thy life.

[Exit EDGAR.*]*

Edmund
  He hath commission from thy wife and me
  To hang Cordelia in the prison, and

To lay the blame upon her own despair,
That she fordid herself.   255

Albany
The gods defend her! Bear him hence awhile.
    [EDMUND *is borne off.*]

[*Enter* LEAR, *with* CORDELIA *dead in his arms;* EDGAR,
    CAPTAIN, *and Others following.*]

Lear
Howl, howl, howl, howl! O, you are men of
    stones!
Had I your tongues and eyes, I'd use them so
That heaven's vault should crack. She's gone for
    ever.
I know when one is dead and when one lives;   260
She's dead as earth. Lend me a looking-glass;
If that her breath will mist or stain the stone,
Why, then she lives.

Kent
                 Is this the promis'd end?

Edgar
Or image of that horror?

Albany
                     Fall and cease!

Lear
This feather stirs; she lives. If it be so,   265
It is a chance which does redeem all sorrows
That ever I have felt.

Kent
              O my good master!

    [*Kneeling.*]

Lear
Prithee away.

Edgar
           'Tis noble Kent, your friend.

Lear
A plague upon you, murderers, traitors all!

270   I might have sav'd her; now she's gone for
        ever.
    Cordelia, Cordelia! stay a little. Ha!
    What is't thou say'st? Her voice was ever soft,
    Gentle, and low – an excellent thing in
        woman.
    I kill'd the slave that was a-hanging thee.

Captain
    'Tis true, my lords, he did.

Lear
275   Did I not, fellow?
    I have seen the day, with my good biting
        falchion,
    I would have made them skip: I am old now,
    And these same crosses spoil me. Who are you?
    Mine eyes are not o' th' best. I'll tell you
        straight.

Kent
280   If fortune brag of two she lov'd and hated,
    One of them we behold.

Lear
    This is a dull sight. Are you not Kent?

Kent
                        The same –
    Your servant Kent. Where is your servant Caius?

Lear
    He's a good fellow, I can tell you that;
285   He'll strike, and quickly too. He's dead and
        rotten.

Kent
    No, my good lord; I am the very man –

Lear
    I'll see that straight.

Kent
    That from your first of difference and decay
    Have follow'd your sad steps.

Lear
                  You are welcome hither.

Kent

Nor no man else! All's cheerless, dark, and deadly.   290
Your eldest daughters have fordone themselves
And desperately are dead.

Lear

                    Ay, so I think.

Albany

He knows not what he says; and vain is it
That we present us to him.

Edgar

                            Very bootless.

[Enter a MESSENGER.*]*

Messenger

Edmund is dead, my lord.

Albany

                    That's but a trifle here.   295
You lords and noble friends, know our intent.
What comfort to this great decay may come
Shall be applied. For us, we will resign
During the life of this old Majesty,
To him our absolute power.
[To EDGAR *and* KENT*]* You to your rights;   300
With boot, and such addition as your honours
Have more than merited. All friends shall taste
The wages of their virtue, and all foes
The cup of their deservings. O, see, see!

Lear

And my poor fool is hang'd! No, no, no life?   305
Why should a dog, a horse, a rat have life,
And thou no breath at all? Thou'lt come no
    more,
Never, never, never, never, never.
Pray you undo this button. Thank you, sir.
Do you see this? Look on her. Look, her lips.   310
Look there, look there!

                [He dies.]

Edgar
     He faints. My lord, my lord!

Kent
 Break, heart; I prithee break.

Edgar
          Look up, my lord,

Kent
 Vex not his ghost. O, let him pass! He hates
  him
 That would upon the rack of this tough world
 Stretch him out longer.

Edgar
315   He is gone indeed.

Kent
 The wonder is he hath endur'd so long:
 He but usurp'd his life.

Albany
 Bear them from hence. Our present business
 Is general woe. *[To* KENT *and* EDGAR*]* Friends of
  my soul, you twain
320 Rule in this realm and the gor'd state sustain.

Kent
 I have a journey, sir, shortly to go.
 My master calls me; I must not say no.

Edgar
 The weight of this sad time we must obey;
 Speak what we feel, not what we ought to say.
325 The oldest hath borne most; we that are young
 Shall never see so much nor live so long.

    [Exeunt with a dead march.]

Shakespeare: Words and Phrases

adapted from the Collins English Dictionary

abate 1 VERB to abate here means to lessen or diminish ❏ *There lives within the very flame of love/A kind of wick or snuff that will abate it* (Hamlet 4.7) 2 VERB to abate here means to shorten ❏ *Abate thy hours* (A Midsummer Night's Dream 3.2) 3 VERB to abate here means to deprive ❏ *She hath abated me of half my train* (King Lear 2.4)

abjure VERB to abjure means to renounce or give up ❏ *this rough magic I here abjure* (Tempest 5.1)

abroad ADV abroad means elsewhere or everywhere ❏ *You have heard of the news abroad* (King Lear 2.1)

abrogate VERB to abrogate means to put an end to ❏ *so it shall praise you to abrogate scurrility* (Love's Labours Lost 4.2)

abuse 1 NOUN abuse in this context means deception or fraud ❏ *What should this mean? Are all the rest come back?/ Or is it some abuse, and no such thing?* (Hamlet 4.7) 2 NOUN an abuse in this context means insult or offence ❏ *I will be deaf to pleading and excuses/Nor tears nor prayers shall purchase our abuses* (Romeo and Juliet 3.1) 3 NOUN an abuse in this context means using something improperly ❏ *we'll digest/ Th'abuse*

of distance (Henry II Chorus) 4 NOUN an abuse in this context means doing something which is corrupt or dishonest ❏ *Come, bring them away: if these be good people in a commonweal that do nothing but their abuses in common houses, I know no law: bring them away.* (Measure for Measure 2.1)

abuser NOUN the abuser here is someone who betrays, a betrayer ❏ *I ... do attach thee/For an abuser of the world* (Othello 1.2)

accent NOUN accent here means language ❏ *In states unborn, and accents yet unknown* (Julius Caesar 3.1)

accident NOUN an accident in this context is an event or something that happened ❏ *think no more of this night's accidents* (A Midsummer Night's Dream 4.1)

accommodate VERB to accommodate in this context means to equip or to give someone the equipment to do something ❏ *The safer sense will ne'er accommodate/His master thus.* (King Lear 4.6)

according ADJ according means sympathetic or ready to agree ❏ *within the scope of choice/Lies*

159

my consent and fair according voice
(Romeo and Juliet 1.2)

account NOUN account often means
judgement (by God) or reckoning
❑ *No reckoning made, but sent to my*
account/ With all my imperfections on
my head (Hamlet 1.5)

accountant ADJ accountant here
means answerable or accountable
❑ *his offence is… /Accountant to the*
law (Measure for Measure 2.4)

ace NOUN ace here means one or first
referring to the lowest score on a dice
❑ *No die, but an ace, for him; for he is*
but one./ Less than an ace, man; for he
is dead; he is nothing. (A Midsummer
Night's Dream 5.1)

acquit VERB here acquit means to be
rid of or free of. It is related to the
verb quit ❑ *I am glad I am so acquit*
of this tinderbox (The Merry Wives of
Windsor 1.3)

afeard ADJ afeard means afraid or
frightened ❑ *Nothing afeard of what*
thyself didst make (Macbeth 1.3)

affiance NOUN affiance means
confidence or trust ❑ *O how hast*
thou with jealousy infected/ The
sweetness of affiance (Henry V 2.2)

affinity NOUN in this context, affinity
means important connections, or
relationships with important people
❑ *The Moor replies/ That he you hurt*
is of great fame in Cyprus,/ And great
affinity (Othello 3.1)

agnize VERB to agnize is an old
word that means that you recognize
or acknowledge something ❑ *I do*
agnize/A natural and prompt alacrity
I find in hardness (Othello 1.3)

ague NOUN an ague is a fever in
which the patient has hot and cold

shivers one after the other ❑ *This*
is some monster of the isle with four
legs, who hath got … an ague (The
Tempest 2.2)

alarm, alarum NOUN an alarm or
alarum is a call to arms or a signal for
soldiers to prepare to fight ❑ *Whence*
cometh this alarum and the noise?
(Henry VI part I 1.4)

Albion NOUN Albion is another
word for England ❑ *but I will sell my*
dukedom,/ To buy a slobbery and a
dirty farm In that nook-shotten isle of
Albion (Henry V 3.5)

all of all PHRASE all of all means
everything, or the sum of all things
❑ *The very all of all (Love's Labours*
Lost 5.1)

amend VERB amend in this context
means to get better or to heal ❑ *at*
his touch… They presently amend
(Macbeth 4.3)

anchor VERB if you anchor on
something you concentrate on it or
fix on it ❑ *My invention … Anchors*
on Isabel (Measure for Measure 2.4)

anon ADV anon was a common word
for soon ❑ *You shall see anon how the*
murderer gets the love of Gonzago's
wife (Hamlet 3.2)

antic 1 ADJ antic here means weird
or strange ❑ *I'll charm the air to give*
a sound/ While you perform your antic
round (Macbeth 4.1) 2 NOUN in
this context antic means a clown or
a strange, unattractive creature ❑ *If*
black, why nature, drawing an antic,/
Made a foul blot (Much Ado About
Nothing 3.1)

apace ADV apace was a common word
for quickly ❑ *Come apace (As You*
Like It 3.3)

apparel NOUN apparel means clothes or clothing ❏ *one suit of apparel* (*Hamlet 3.2*)

appliance NOUN appliance here means cure ❏ *Diseases desperate grown/By desperate appliance are relieved* (*Hamlet 4.3*)

argument NOUN argument here means a topic of conversation or the subject ❏ *Why 'tis the rarest argument of wonder that hath shot out in our latter times* (*All's Well That Ends Well 2.3*)

arrant ADJ arrant means absolute, complete. It strengthens the meaning of a noun ❏ *Fortune, that arrant whore* (*King Lear 2.4*)

arras NOUN an arras is a tapestry, a large cloth with a picture sewn on it using coloured thread ❏ *Behind the arras I'll convey myself/To hear the process* (*Hamlet 3.3*)

art 1 NOUN art in this context means knowledge ❏ *Their malady convinces/The great essay of art* (*Macbeth 4.3*) 2 NOUN art can also mean skill as it does here ❏ *He ... gave you such a masterly report/For art and exercise in your defence* (*Hamlet 4.7*) 3 NOUN art here means magic ❏ *Now I want/Spirits to enforce, art to enchant* (*The Tempest 5 Epilogue*)

assay 1 NOUN an assay was an attempt, a try ❏ *Make assay./Bow, stubborn knees* (*Hamlet 3.3*) 2 NOUN assay can also mean a test or a trial ❏ *he hath made assay of her virtue* (*Measure for Measure 3.1*)

attend (on/upon) VERB attend on means to wait for or to expect ❏ *Tarry I here, I but attend on death* (*Two Gentlemen of Verona 3.1*)

auditor NOUN an auditor was a member of an audience or someone who listens ❏ *I'll be an auditor* (*A Midsummer Night's Dream 3.1*)

aught NOUN aught was a common word which meant anything ❏ *if my love thou holdest at aught* (*Hamlet 4.3*)

aunt 1 NOUN an aunt was another word for an old woman and also means someone who talks a lot or a gossip ❏ *The wisest aunt telling the saddest tale* (*A Midsummer Night's Dream 2.1*) 2 NOUN aunt could also mean a mistress or a prostitute ❏ *the thrush and the jay/Are summer songs for me and my aunts/While we lie tumbling in the hay* (*The Winter's Tale 4.3*)

avaunt EXCLAM avaunt was a common word which meant go away ❏ *Avaunt, you curs!* (*King Lear 3.6*)

aye ADV here aye means always or ever ❏ *Whose state and honour I for aye allow* (*Richard II 5.2*)

baffle VERB baffle meant to be disgraced in public or humiliated ❏ *I am disgraced, impeached, and baffled here* (*Richard II 1.1*)

bald ADJ bald means trivial or silly ❏ *I knew 'twould be a bald conclusion* (*The Comedy of Errors 2.2*)

ban NOUN a ban was a curse or an evil spell ❏ *Sometimes with lunatic bans... Enforce their charity* (*King Lear 2.3*)

barren ADJ barren meant empty or hollow ❏ *now I let go your hand, I am barren.* (*Twelfth Night 1.3*)

base ADJ base is an adjective that means unworthy or dishonourable ❏ *civet is of a baser birth than tar* (*As You Like It 3.2*)

161

base 1 ADJ base can also mean of low social standing or someone who was not part of the ruling class ❑ *Why brand they us with 'base'?* (*King Lear 1.2*) 2 ADJ here base means poor quality ❑ *Base cousin,/ Darest thou break first?* (*Two Noble Kinsmen 3.3*)

bawdy NOUN bawdy means obscene or rude ❑ *Bloody, bawdy villain!* (*Hamlet 2.2*)

bear in hand PHRASE bear in hand means taken advantage of or fooled ❑ *This I made good to you In our last conference, passed in probation with you/ How you were borne in hand* (*Macbeth 3.1*)

beard VERB to beard someone was to oppose or confront them ❑ *Com'st thou to beard me in Denmark?* (*Hamlet 2.2*)

beard, in one's PHRASE if you say something in someone's beard you say it to their face ❑ *I will verify as much in his beard* (*Henry V 3.2*)

beaver NOUN a beaver was a visor on a battle helmet ❑ *O yes, my lord, he wore his beaver up* (*Hamlet 1.2*)

become VERB if something becomes you it suits you or is appropriate to you ❑ *Nothing in his life became him like the leaving it* (*Macbeth 1.4*)

bed, brought to PHRASE to be brought to bed means to give birth ❑ *His wife but yesternight was brought to bed* (*Titus Andronicus 4.2*)

bedabbled ADJ if something is bedabbled it is sprinkled ❑ *Bedabbled with the dew, and torn with briers* (*A Midsummer Night's Dream 3.2*)

Bedlam NOUN Bedlam was a word used for Bethlehem Hospital which was a place the insane were sent to ❑ *The country give me proof and precedent/ Of Bedlam beggars* (*King Lear 2.3*)

bed-swerver NOUN a bed-swerver was someone who was unfaithful in marriage, an adulterer ❑ *she's/A bed-swerver* (*Winter's Tale 2.1*)

befall 1 VERB to befall is to happen, occur or take place ❑ *In this same interlude it doth befall/ That I present a wall* (*A Midsummer Night's Dream 5.1*) 2 VERB to befall can also mean to happen to someone or something ❑ *fair befall thee and thy noble house* (*Richard III 1.3*)

behoof NOUN behoof was an advantage or benefit ❑ *All our surgeons/ Convent in their behoof* (*Two Noble Kinsmen 1.4*)

beldam NOUN a beldam was a witch or old woman ❑ *Have I not reason, beldams as you are?* (*Macbeth 3.5*)

belike ADV belike meant probably, perhaps or presumably ❑ *belike he likes it not* (*Hamlet 3.2*)

bent 1 NOUN bent means a preference or a direction ❑ *Let me work,/ For I can give his humour true bent,/ And I will bring him to the Capitol* (*Julius Caesar 2.1*) 2 ADJ if you are bent on something you are determined to do it ❑ *for now I am bent to know/ By the worst means the worst.* (*Macbeth 3.4*)

beshrew VERB beshrew meant to curse or wish evil on someone ❑ *much beshrew my manners and my pride/ If Hermia meant to say Lysander lied* (*A Midsummer Night's Dream 2.2*)

betime (s) ADV betime means early ❑ *To business that we love we rise betime* (Antony and Cleopatra 4.4)

bevy NOUN bevy meant type or sort, it was also used to mean company ❑ *many more of the same bevy* (Hamlet 5.2)

blazon VERB to blazon something meant to display or show it ❑ *that thy skill be more to blazon it* (Romeo and Juliet 2.6)

blind ADJ if you are blind when you do something you are reckless or do not care about the consequences ❑ *are you yet to your own souls so blind/That two you will war with God by murdering me* (Richard III 1.4)

bombast NOUN bombast was wool stuffing (used in a cushion for example) and so it came to mean padded out or long-winded. Here it means someone who talks a lot about nothing in particular ❑ *How now my sweet creature of bombast* (Henry IV part I 2.4)

bond 1 NOUN a bond is a contract or legal deed ❑ *Well, then, your bond, and let me see* (Merchant of Venice 1.3) 2 NOUN bond could also mean duty or commitment ❑ *I love your majesty/According to my bond* (King Lear 1.1)

bottom NOUN here bottom means essence, main point or intent ❑ *Now I see/The bottom of your purpose* (All's Well That Ends Well 3.7)

bounteously ADV bounteously means plentifully, abundantly ❑ *I prithee, and I'll pay thee bounteously* (Twelfth Night 1.2)

brace 1 NOUN a brace is a couple or two ❑ *Have lost a brace of kinsmen* (Romeo and Juliet 5.3) 2 NOUN if you are in a brace position it means you are ready ❑ *For that it stands not in such warlike brace* (Othello 1.3)

brand VERB to mark permanantly like the markings on cattle ❑ *the wheeled seat/Of fortunate Caesar ... branded his baseness that ensued* (Anthony and Cleopatra 4.14)

brave ADJ brave meant fine, excellent or splendid ❑ *O brave new world/That has such people in't* (The Tempest 5.1)

brine NOUN brine is sea-water ❑ *He shall drink nought brine, for I'll not show him/Where the quick freshes are* (The Tempest 3.2)

brow NOUN brow in this context means appearance ❑ *doth hourly grow/Out of his brows* (Hamlet 3.3)

burden 1 NOUN the burden here is a chorus ❑ *I would sing my song without a burden* (As You Like It 3.2) 2 NOUN burden means load or weight (this is the current meaning) ❑ *the scarfs and the bannerets about thee did manifoldly dissuade me from believing thee a vessel of too great a burden* (All's Well that Ends Well 2.3)

buttons, in one's PHRASE this is a phrase that means clear, easy to see ❑ *Tis in his buttons he will carry't* (The Merry Wives of Windsor 3.2)

cable NOUN cable here means scope or reach ❑ *The law ... Will give her cable* (Othello 1.2)

cadent ADJ if something is cadent it is falling or dropping ❑ *With cadent tears fret channels in her cheeks* (King Lear 1.4)

canker VERB to canker is to decay, become corrupt ❏ *And, as with age his body uglier grows,/So his mind cankers* (*The Tempest 4.1*)

canon, from the PHRASE from the canon is an expression meaning out of order, improper ❏ *Twas from the canon* (*Coriolanus 3.1*)

cap-a-pie ADV cap-a-pie means from head to foot, completely ❏ *I am courtier cap-a-pie* (*The Winter's Tale 4.4*)

carbonadoed ADJ if something is carbonadoed it is cut or scored (scratched) with a knife ❏ *it is your carbonadoed* (*All's Well That Ends Well 4.5*)

carouse VERB to carouse is to drink at length, party ❏ *They cast their caps up and carouse together* (*Anthony and Cleopatra 4.12*)

carrack NOUN a carrack was a large old ship, a galleon ❏ *Faith, he tonight hath boarded a land-carrack* (*Othello 1.2*)

cassock NOUN a cassock here means a military cloak, long coat ❏ *half of the which dare not shake the snow from off their cassocks lest they shake themselves to pieces* (*All's Well That Ends Well 4.3*)

catastrophe NOUN catastrophe here means conclusion or end ❏ *pat he comes, like the catastrophe of the old comedy* (*King Lear 1.2*)

cautel NOUN a cautel was a trick or a deceptive act ❏ *Perhaps he loves you now/And now no soil not cautel doth besmirch* (*Hamlet 1.2*)

celerity NOUN celerity was a common word for speed, swiftness ❏ *Hence hath offence his quick celerity/When it is borne in high authority* (*Measure for Measure 4.2*)

chafe NOUN chafe meant anger or temper ❏ *this Herculean Roman does become/The carriage of his chafe* (*Anthony and Cleopatra 1.3*)

chanson NOUN chanson was an old word for a song ❏ *The first row of the pious chanson will show you more* (*Hamlet 2.2*)

chapman NOUN a chapman was a trader or merchant ❏ *Not uttered by base sale of chapman's tongues* (*Love's Labours Lost 2.1*)

chaps, chops NOUN chaps (and chops) was a word for jaws ❏ *Which ne'er shook hands nor bade farewell to him/Till he unseamed him from the nave to th' chops* (*Macbeth 1.2*)

chattels NOUN chattels were your moveable possessions. The word is used in the traditional marriage ceremony ❏ *She is my goods, my chattels* (*The Taming of the Shrew 3.3*)

chide VERB if you are chided by someone you are told off or reprimanded ❏ *Now I but chide, but I should use thee worse* (*A Midsummer Night's Dream 3.2*)

chinks NOUN chinks was a word for cash or money ❏ *he that can lay hold of her/Shall have the chinks* (*Romeo and Juliet 1.5*)

choleric ADJ if something was called choleric it meant that they were quick to get angry ❏ *therewithal unruly waywardness that infirm and choleric years bring with them* (*King Lear 1.1*)

chuff NOUN a chuff was a miser,

someone who clings to his or her money ❑ *ye fat chuffs* (*Henry IV part I 2.2*)

cipher NOUN cipher here means nothing ❑ *Mine were the very cipher of a function* (*Measure for Measure 2.2*)

circummured ADJ circummured means that something is surrounded with a wall ❑ *He hath a garden circummured with brick* (*Measure for Measure 4.1*)

civet NOUN a civet is a type of scent or perfume ❑ *Give me an ounce of civet* (*King Lear 4.6*)

clamorous ADJ clamorous means noisy or boisterous ❑ *Be clamorous and leap all civil bounds* (*Twelfth Night 1.4*)

clangour, clangor NOUN clangour is a word that means ringing (the sound that bells make) ❑ *Like to a dismal clangour heard from far* (*Henry VI part III 2.3*)

cleave VERB if you cleave to something you stick to it or are faithful to it ❑ *Thy thoughts I cleave to* (*The Tempest 4.1*)

clock and clock, 'twixt PHRASE from hour to hour, without stopping or continuously ❑ *To weep 'twixt clock and clock* (*Cymbeline 3.4*)

close ADJ here close means hidden ❑ *Stand close; this is the same Athenian* (*A Midsummer Night's Dream 3.2*)

cloud NOUN a cloud on your face means that you have a troubled, unhappy expression ❑ *He has cloud in's face* (*Anthony and Cleopatra 3.2*)

cloy VERB if you cloy an appetite you satisfy it ❑ *Other women cloy/The appetites they feed* (*Anthony and Cleopatra 2.2*)

cock-a-hoop, set PHRASE if you set cock-a-hoop you become free of everything ❑ *You will set cock-a-hoop* (*Romeo and Juliet 1.5*)

colours NOUN colours is a word used to describe battle-flags or banners. Sometimes we still say that we nail our colours to the mast if we are stating which team or side of an argument we support ❑ *the approbation of those that weep this lamentable divorce under her colours* (*Cymbeline 1.5*)

combustion NOUN combustion was a word meaning disorder or chaos ❑ *prophesying ... Of dire combustion and confused events* (*Macbeth 2.3*)

comely ADJ if you are or something is comely you or it is lovely, beautiful, graceful ❑ *O, what a world is this, when what is comely/Envenoms him that bears it!* (*As You Like It 2.3*)

commend VERB if you commend yourself to someone you send greetings to them ❑ *Commend me to my brother* (*Measure for Measure 1.4*)

compact NOUN a compact is an agreement or a contract ❑ *what compact mean you to have with us?* (*Julius Caesar 3.1*)

compass 1 NOUN here compass means range or scope ❑ *you would sound me from my lowest note to the top of my compass* (*Hamlet 3.2*) 2 VERB to compass here means to achieve, bring about or make happen ❑ *How now shall this be compassed?/ Canst thou bring me to the party?* (*Tempest 3.2*)

comptible ADJ comptible is an old word meaning sensitive ❑ *I am very comptible, even to the least sinister usage.* (*Twelfth Night 1.5*)

confederacy NOUN a confederacy is a group of people usually joined together to commit a crime. It is another word for a conspiracy ❑ *Lo, she is one of this confederacy!* (*A Midsummer Night's Dream 3.2*)

confound VERB if you confound something you confuse it or mix it up; it also means to stop or prevent ❑ *A million fail, confounding oath on oath.* (*A Midsummer Night's Dream 3.2*)

contagion NOUN contagion is an old word for disease or poison ❑ *hell itself breathes out/ Contagion to this world* (*Hamlet 3.2*)

contumely NOUN contumely is an old word for an insult ❑ *the proud man's contumely* (*Hamlet 3.1*)

counterfeit 1 VERB if you counterfeit something you copy or imitate it ❑ *Meantime your cheeks do counterfeit our roses* (*Henry VI part I 2.4*) 2 VERB in this context counterfeit means to pretend or make believe ❑ *I will counterfeit the bewitchment of some popular man* (*Coriolanus*)

coz NOUN coz was a shortened form of the word cousin ❑ *sweet my coz, be merry* (*As You Like It 1.2*)

cozenage NOUN cozenage is an old word meaning cheating or a deception ❑ *Thrown out his angle for my proper life,/ And with such coz'nage* (*Hamlet 5.2*)

crave VERB crave used to mean to beg or request ❑ *I crave your pardon* (*The Comedy of Errors 1.2*)

crotchet NOUN crotchets are strange ideas or whims ❑ *thou hast some strange crotchets in thy head now* (*The Merry Wives of Windsor 2.1*)

cuckold NOUN a cuckold is a man whose wife has been unfaithful to him ❑ *As there is no true cuckold but calamity* (*Twelfth Night 1.5*)

cuffs, go to PHRASE this phrase meant to fight ❑ *the player went to cuffs in the question* (*Hamlet 2.2*)

cup VERB in this context cup is a verb which means to pour drink or fill glasses with alcohol ❑ *cup us til the world go round* (*Anthony and Cleopatra 2.7*)

cur NOUN cur is an insult meaning dog and is also used to mean coward ❑ *Out, dog! out, cur! Thou drivest me past the bounds/ Of maiden's patience* (*A Midsummer Night's Dream 3.2*)

curiously ADV in this context curiously means carefully or skilfully ❑ *The sleeves curiously cut* (*The Taming of the Shrew 4.3*)

curry VERB curry means to flatter or to praise someone more than they are worth ❑ *I would curry with Master Shallow that no man could better command his servants* (*Henry IV part II 5.1*)

custom NOUN custom is a habit or a usual practice ❑ *Hath not old custom made this life more sweet/ Than that of painted pomp?* (*As You Like It 2.1*)

cutpurse NOUN a cutpurse is an old word for a thief. Men used to carry their money in small bags (purse) that hung from their belts; thieves would cut the purse from the belt and steal their money ❑ *A cutpurse of the empire and the rule* (*Hamlet 3.4*)

dainty ADJ dainty used to mean splendid, fine ❑ *Why, that's my dainty Ariel!* (Tempest 5.1)

dally VERB if you dally with something you play with it or tease it ❑ *They that dally nicely with words may quickly make them wanton* (Twelfth Night 3.1)

damask COLOUR damask is a light-red or pink colour ❑ *'Twas just the difference/Betwixt the constant red and mingled damask* (As You Like It 3.5)

dare 1 VERB dare means to challeng or, confront ❑ *He goes before me, and still dares me on* (A Midsummer Night's Dream 3.3) 2 VERB dare in this context means to present, deliver or inflict ❑ *all that fortune, death, and danger dare* (Hamlet 4.4)

darkly ADV darkly was used in this context to mean secretly or cunningly ❑ *I will go darkly to work with her* (Measure for Measure 5.1)

daw NOUN a daw was a slang term for idiot or fool (after the bird jackdaw which was famous for its stupidity) ❑ *Yea, just so much as you may take upon a knife's point and choke a daw withal* (Much Ado About Nothing 3.1)

debile ADJ debile meant weak or feeble ❑ *And debile minister great power* (All's Well That Ends Well 2.3)

deboshed ADJ deboshed was another way of saying corrupted or debauched ❑ *Men so disordered, deboshed and bold* (King Lear 1.4)

decoct VERB to decoct was to heat up, warm something ❑ *Can sodden water,/A drench for sur-reained jades*

... Decoct their cold blood to such valiant heat? (Henry V 3.5)

deep-revolving ADJ deep-revolving here uses the idea that you turn something over in your mind when you are thinking hard about it and so means deep-thinking, meditating ❑ *The deep-revolving Buckingham/No more shall be the neighbour to my counsels* (Richard III 4.2)

defect NOUN defect here means shortcoming or something that is not right ❑ *Being unprepared/Our will became the servant to defect* (Macbeth 2.1)

degree 1 NOUN degree here means rank, standing or station ❑ *Should a like language use to all degrees,/And mannerly distinguishment leave out/Betwixt the prince and beggar* (The Winter's Tale 2.1) 2 NOUN in this context, degree means extent or measure ❑ *her offence/Must be of such unnatural degree* (King Lear 1.1)

deify VERB if you deify something or someone you worship it or them as a God ❑ *all.. deifying the name of Rosalind* (As You Like It 3.2)

delated ADJ delated here means detailed ❑ *the scope/Of these delated articles* (Hamlet 1.2)

delicate ADJ if something was described as delicate it meant it was of fine quality or valuable ❑ *thou wast a spirit too delicate* (The Tempest 1.2)

demise VERB in this context demise means to transmit, give or convey ❑ *what state ... Canst thou demise to any child of mine?* (Richard III 4.4)

deplore VERB to deplore means to express with grief or sorrow ❑ *Never more/ Will I my master's tears to you deplore* (*Twelfth Night 3.1*)

depose VERB if you depose someone you make them take an oath, or swear something to be true ❑ *Depose him in the justice of his cause* (*Richard II 1.3*)

depositary NOUN a depositary is a trustee ❑ *Made you ... my depositary* (*King Lear 2.4*)

derive 1 VERB to derive means to comes from or to descend (it usually applies to people) ❑ *No part of it is mine,/ This shame derives itself from unknown loins.* (*Much Ado About Nothing 4.1*) 2 VERB if you derive something from someone you inherit it ❑ *Treason is not inherited ...Or, if we derive it from our friends/ What's that to me?* (*As You Like It 1.3*)

descry VERB to see or catch sight of ❑ *The news is true, my lord. He is descried* (*Anthony and Cleopatra 3.7*)

desert 1 NOUN desert means worth or merit ❑ *That dost in vile misproson shackle up/ My love and her desert* (*All's Well That Ends Well 2.3*) 2 ADJ desert is used here to mean lonely or isolated ❑ *if that love or gold/ Can in this desert place buy entertainment* (*As You LIke It 2.4*)

design 1 VERB to design means to indicate or point out ❑ *we shall see/ Justice design the victor's chivalry* (*Richard II 1.1*) 2 NOUN a design is a plan, an intention or an undertaking ❑ *hinder not the honour of his design* (*All's Well That Ends Well 3.6*)

designment NOUN a designment was a plan or undertaking ❑ *The desperate tempest hath so bang'd the Turks,/ That their designment halts* (*Othello 2.1*)

despite VERB despite here means to spite or attempt to thwart a plan ❑ *Only to despite them I will endeavour anything* (*Much Ado About Nothing 2.2*)

device NOUN a device is a plan, plot or trick ❑ *Excellent, I smell a device* (*Twelfth Night 2.3*)

disable VERB to disable here means to devalue or make little of ❑ *he disabled my judgement* (*As You Like It 5.4*)

discandy VERB here discandy means to melt away or dissolve ❑ *The hearts ... do discandy , melt their sweets* (*Anthony and Cleopatra 4.12*)

disciple VERB to disciple is to teach or train ❑ *He ...was/ Discipled of the bravest* (*All's Well That Ends Well 1.2*)

discommend VERB if you discommend something you criticize it ❑ *my dialect which you discommend so much* (*King Lear 2.2*)

discourse NOUN discourse means conversation, talk or chat ❑ *which part of it I'll waste/ With such discourse as I not doubt shall make it/ Go quick away* (*The Tempest 5.1*)

discover VERB discover used to mean to reveal or show ❑ *the Prince discovered to Claudio that he loved my niece* (*Much Ado About Nothing 1.2*)

disliken VERB disguise, make unlike ❑ *disliken/ The truth of your own seeming* (*The Winter's Tale 4.4*)

dismantle VERB to dismantle is to remove or take away ❑ *Commit a thing so monstrous to dismantle/*

So many folds of favour (*King Lear 1.1*)

disponge VERB disponge means to pour out or rain down ❑ *The poisonous damp of night disponge upon me* (*Anthony and Cleopatra 4.9*)

distrain VERB to distrain something is to confiscate it ❑ *My father's goods are all distrained and sold* (*Richard II 2.3*)

divers ADJ divers is an old word for various ❑ *I will give out divers schedules of my beauty* (*Twelfth Night 1.5*)

doff VERB to doff is to get rid of or dispose ❑ *make our women fight/To doff their dire distresses* (*Macbeth 4.3*)

dog VERB if you dog someone or something you follow them or it closely ❑ *I will rather leave to see Hector than not to dog him* (*Troilus and Cressida 5.1*)

dotage NOUN dotage here means infatuation ❑ *Her dotage now I do begin to pity* (*A Midsummer NIght's Dream 4.1*)

dotard NOUN a dotard was an old fool ❑ *I speak not like a dotard nor a fool* (*Much Ado About Nothing 5.1*)

dote VERB to dote is to love, cherish, care without seeing any fault ❑ *And won her soul; and she, sweet lady, dotes,/Devoutly dotes, dotes in idolatry* (*A Midsummer Night's Dream 1.1*)

doublet NOUN a doublet was a man's close-fitting jacket with short skirt ❑ *Lord Hamlet, with his doublet all unbraced* (*Hamlet 2.1*)

dowager NOUN a dowager is a widow ❑ *Like to a step-dame or a dowage* (*A Midsummer Night's Dream 1.1*)

dowdy NOUN a dowdy was an ugly woman ❑ *Dido was a dowdy* (*Romeo and Juliet 2.4*)

dower NOUN a dower (or dowery) is the riches or property given by the father of a bride to her husband-to-be ❑ *Thy truth then by they dower* (*King Lear 1.1*)

dram NOUN a dram is a tiny amount ❑ *Why, everything adheres together that no dram of a scruple* (*Twelfth Night 3.4*)

drift NOUN drift is a plan, scheme or intention ❑ *Shall Romeo by my letters know our drift* (*Romeo and Juliet 4.1*)

dropsied ADJ dropsied means pretentious ❑ *Where great additions swell's and virtues none/It is a dropsied honour* (*All's Well That Ends Well 2.3*)

drudge NOUN a drudge was a slave, servant ❑ *If I be his cuckold, he's my drudge* (*All's Well That Ends Well 1.3*)

dwell VERB to dwell sometimes meant to exist, to be ❑ *I'd rather dwell in my necessity* (*Merchant of Venice 1.3*)

earnest ADJ an earnest was a pledge to pay or a payment in advance ❑ *for an earnest of a greater honour/He bade me from him call thee Thane of Cawdor* (*Macbeth 1.3*)

ecstasy NOUN madness ❑ *This is the very ecstasy of love* (*Hamlet 2.1*)

edict NOUN law or declaration ❑ *It stands as an edict in destiny.* (*A Midsummer Night's Dream 1.1*)

169

egall ADJ egall is an old word meaning equal ❑ *companions/ Whose souls do bear an egall yoke of love* (Merchant of Venice 2.4)

eisel NOUN eisel meant vinegar ❑ *Woo't drink up eisel?* (Hamlet 5.1)

eke, eke out VERB eke meant to add to, to increase. Eke out nowadays means to make something last as long as possible – particularly in the sense of making money last a long time ❑ *Still be kind/ And eke out our performance with your mind* (Henry V Chorus)

elbow, out at PHRASE out at elbow is an old phrase meaning in poor condition – as when your jacket sleeves are worn at the elbow which shows that it is an old jacket ❑ *He cannot, sir. He's out at elbow* (Measure for Measure 2.1)

element NOUN elements were thought to be the things from which all things were made. They were: air, earth, water and fire ❑ *Does not our lives consist of the four elements?* (Twelfth Night 2.3)

elf VERB to elf was to tangle ❑ *I'll ... elf all my hairs in knots* (King Lear 2.3)

embassy NOUN an embassy was a message ❑ *We'll once more hear Orsino's embassy.* (Twelfth Night 1.5)

emphasis NOUN emphasis here means a forceful expression or strong statement ❑ *What is he whose grief/ Bears such an emphasis* (Hamlet 5.1)

empiric NOUN an empiric was an untrained doctor sometimes called a quack ❑ *we must not ... prostitute our past-cure malady/ To empirics* (All's Well That Ends Well 2.1)

emulate ADJ emulate here means envious ❑ *pricked on by a most emulate pride* (Hamlet 1.1)

enchant VERB to enchant meant to put a magic spell on ❑ *Damn'd as thou art, thou hast enchanted her,/ For I'll refer me to all things of sense* (Othello 1.2)

enclog VERB to enclog was to hinder something or to provide an obstacle to it ❑ *Traitors enscarped to enclog the guitless keel* (Othello 1.2)

endure VERB to endure was to allow or to permit ❑ *and will endure/ Our setting down before't.* (Macbeth 5.4)

enfranchise VERB if you enfranchised something you set it free ❑ *Do this or this;/ Take in that kingdom and enfranchise that;/ Perform't, or else we damn thee.'* (Anthony and Cleopatra 1.1)

engage VERB to engage here means to pledge or to promise ❑ *This to be true I do engage my life* (As You Like It 5.4)

engaol VERB to lock up or put in prison ❑ *Within my mouth you have engaoled my tongue* (Richard II 1.3)

engine NOUN an engine was a plot, device or a machine ❑ *their promises, enticements, oaths, tokens, and all these engines, of lust, are not the things they go under* (All's Well That Ends Well 3.5)

englut VERB if you were engulfed you were swallowed up or eaten whole ❑ *For certainly thou art so near the gulf,/ Thou needs must be englutted.* (Henry V 4.3)

enjoined ADJ enjoined describes people joined together for the same reason ❑ *Of enjoined penitents/*

There's four or five (All's Well That Ends Well 3.5)

entertain 1 VERB to entertain here means to welcome or receive □ *Approach, rich Ceres, her to entertain. (The Tempest 4.1)* 2 VERB to entertain in this context means to cherish, hold in high regard or to respect □ *and I quake,/ Lest thou a feverous life shouldst entertain/ And six or seven winters more respect/ Than a perpetual honour. (Measure for Measure 3.1)* 3 VERB to entertain means here to give something consideration □ *But entertain it,/ And though you think me poor, I am the man/ Will give thee all the world. (Anthony and Cleopatra 2.7)* 4 VERB to entertain here means to treat or handle □ *your highness is not entertained with that ceremonious affection as you were wont (King Lear 1.4)*

envious ADJ envious meant spiteful or vindictive □ *he shall appear to the envious a scholar (Measure for Measure 3.2)*

ere PREP ere was a common word for before □ *ere this I should ha' fatted all the region kites (Hamlet 2.2)*

err VERB to err means to go astray, to make a mistake □ *And as he errs, doting on Hermia's eyes (A Midsummer Night's Dream 1.1)*

erst ADV erst was a common word for once or before □ *that erst brought sweetly forth/ The freckled cowslip (Henry V 5.2)*

eschew VERB if you eschew something you deliberately avoid doing it □ *What cannot be eschewed must be embraced (The Merry Wives of Windsor 5.5)*

escote VERB to escote meant to pay for, support □ *How are they escoted? (Hamlet 2.2)*

estimable ADJ estimable meant appreciative □ *I could not with such estimable wonder over-far believe that (Twelfth Night 2.1)*

extenuate VERB extenuate means to lessen □ *Which by no means we may extenuate (A Midsummer Night's Dream 1.1)*

fain ADV fain was a common word meaning gladly or willingly □ *I would fain prove so (Hamlet 2.2)*

fall NOUN in a voice or music fall meant going higher and lower □ *and so die/ That strain again! it had a dying fall (Twelfth Night 1.1)*

false ADJ false was a common word for treacherous □ *this is counter, you false Danish dogs! (Hamlet 4.5)*

fare VERB fare means to get on or manage □ *I fare well (The Taming of the Shrew Introduction 2)*

feign VERB to feign was to make up, pretend or fake □ *It is the more like to be feigned (Twelfth Night 1.5)*

fie EXCLAM fie was an exclamation of disgust □ *Fie, that you'll say so! (Twelfth Night 1.3)*

figure VERB to figure was to symbolize or look like □ *Wings and no eyes, figure unheedy haste (A Midsummer Night's Dream 1.1)*

filch VERB if you filch something you steal it □ *With cunning hast thou filch'd my daughter's heart (A Midsummer Night's Dream 1.1)*

flout VERB to flout something meant to scorn it □ *Why will you suffer her to flout me thus? (A Midsummer Night's Dream 3.2)*

171

fond ADJ fond was a common word meaning foolish ☐ *Shall we their fond pageant see? (A Midsummer Night's Dream 3.2)*

footing 1 NOUN footing meant landing on shore, arrival, disembarkation ☐ *Whose footing here anticipates our thoughts/A se'nnight's speed. (Othello 2.1)* 2 NOUN footing also means support ☐ *there your charity would have lacked footing (Winter's Tale 3.3)*

forsooth ADV in truth, certainly, truly
☐ *I had rather, forsooth, go before you like a man (The Merry Wives of Windsor 3.2)*

forswear VERB if you forswear you lie, swear falsely or break your word ☐ *he swore a thing to me on Monday night, which he forswore on Tuesday morning (Much Ado About Nothing 5.1)*

freshes NOUN a fresh is a fresh water stream ☐ *He shall drink nought brine, for I'll not show him/Where the quick freshes are. (Tempest 3.2)*

furlong NOUN a furlong is a measure of distance. It is the equivalent on one eight of a mile ☐ *Now would I give a thousand furlongs of sea for an acre of barren ground (Tempest 1.1)*

gaberdine NOUN a gaberdine is a cloak ☐ *My best way is to creep under his gaberdine (Tempest 2.2)*

gage NOUN a gage was a challenge to duel or fight ☐ *There is my gage, Aumerle, in gage to thine (Richard II 4.1)*

gait NOUN your gait is your way of walking or step ☐ *I know her by her gait (Tempest 4.1)*

gall VERB to gall is to annoy or irritate ☐ *Let it not gall your patience, good Iago,/That I extend my manners (Othello 2.1)*

gambol NOUN frolic or play ☐ *Hop in his walks, and gambol in his eyes (A Midsummer Night's Dream 3.1)*

gaskins NOUN gaskins is an old word for trousers ☐ *or, if both break, your gaskins fall. (Twelfth Night 1.5)*

gentle ADJ gentle means noble or well-born ☐ *thrice-gentle Cassio! (Othello 3.4)*

glass NOUN a glass was another word for a mirror ☐ *no woman's face remember/Save from my glass, mine own (Tempest 3.1)*

gleek VERB to gleek means to make a joke or jibe ☐ *Nay, I can gleek upon occasion (A Midsummer Night's Dream 3.1)*

gust NOUN gust meant taste, desire or enjoyment. We still say that if you do something with gusto you do it with enjoyment or enthusiasm ☐ *the gust he hath in quarrelling (Twelfth Night 1.3)*

habit NOUN habit means clothes ☐ *You know me by my habit (Henry V 3.6)*

heaviness NOUN heaviness means sadness or grief ☐ *So sorrow's heaviness doth heavier grow/For debt that bankrupt sleep doth sorrow owe (A Midsummer Night's Dream 3.2)*

heavy ADJ if you are heavy you are said to be sad or sorrowful ☐ *Away from light steals home my heavy son (Romeo and Juliet 1.1)*

hie VERB to hie meant to hurry ☐ *My husband hies him home (All Well That Ends Well 4.4)*

hollowly ADV if you did something hollowly you did it insincerely ❏ *If hollowly invert/What best is boded me to mischief!* (Tempest 3.1)

holy-water, court PHRASE if you court holy water you make empty promises, or make statements which sound good but have no real meaning ❏ *court holy-water in a dry house is better than this rain-water out o'door* (King Lear 3.2)

howsoever ADV howsoever was often used instead of however ❏ *But howsoever strange and admirable* (A Midsummer Night's Dream 5.1)

humour NOUN your humour was your mood, frame of mind or temperament ❏ *it fits my humour well* (As You Like It 3.2)

ill ADJ ill means bad ❏ *I must thank him only,/Let my remembrance suffer ill report* (Antony and Cleopatra 2.2)

indistinct ADJ inseparable or unable to see a difference ❏ *Even till we make the main and the aerial blue/An indistinct regard.* (Othello 2.1)

indulgence NOUN indulgence meant approval ❏ *As you from crimes would pardoned be,/Let your indulgence set me free* (The Tempest Epilogue)

infirmity NOUN infirmity was weakness or fraility ❏ *Be not disturbed with my infirmity* (The Tempest 4.1)

intelligence NOUN here intelligence means information ❏ *Pursue her; and for this intelligence/If I have thanks* (A Midsummer Night's Dream 1.1)

inwards NOUN inwards meant someone's internal organs ❏ *the thought whereof/Doth like a poisonous mineral gnaw my inwards* (Othello 2.1)

issue 1 NOUN the issue of a marriage are the children ❏ *To thine and Albany's issues,/Be this perpetual* (King Lear 1.1) 2 NOUN in this context issue means outcome or result ❏ *I am to pray you, not to strain my speech,/To grosser issues* (Othello)

kind NOUN kind here means situation or case ❏ *But in this kind, wanting your father's voice,/The other must be held the worthier.* (A Midsummer Night's Dream 1.1)

knave NOUN a knave was a common word for scoundrel ❏ *How absolute the knave is!* (Hamlet 5.1)

league NOUN A distance. A league was the distance a person could walk in one hour ❏ *From Athens is her house remote seven leagues* (A Midsummer Night's Dream 1.1)

lief, had as ADJ I had as lief means I should like just as much ❏ *I had as lief the town crier spoke my lines* (Hamlet 1.2)

livery NOUN livery was a costume, outfit, uniform usually worn by a servant ❏ *You can endure the livery of a nun* (A Midsummer Night's Dream 1.1)

loam NOUN loam is soil containing decayed vegetable matter and therefore good for growing crops and plants ❏ *and let him have some plaster, or some loam, or some rough-cast about him, to signify wall* (A Midsummer Night's Dream 3.1)

lusty ADJ lusty meant strong ❏ *and oared/Himself with his good arms in lusty stroke/To th' shore* (The Tempest 2.1)

maidenhead NOUN maidenhead
means chastity or virginity ❑ *What I
am, and what I would, are as secret as
maidenhead* (*Twelfth Night 1.5*)

mark VERB mark means to note or
pay attention to ❑ *Where sighs and
groans,/
Are made not marked* (*Macbeth 4.3*)

marvellous ADJ very or extremely
❑ *here's a marvellous convenient place
for our rehearsal* (*A Midsummer
Night's Dream 3.1*)

meet ADJ right or proper ❑ *tis most
meet you should* (*Macbeth 5.1*)

merely ADV completely or entirely
❑ *Love is merely a madness* (*As You
Like It 3.2*)

misgraffed ADJ misgraffed is an
old word for mismatched or unequal
❑ *Or else misgraffed in respect
of years* (*A Midsummer Night's
Dream 1.1*)

misprision NOUN a misprision
meant an error or mistake
❑ *Misprision in the highest degree!*
(*Twelfth Night 1.5*)

mollification NOUN mollification is
appeasement or a way of preventing
someone getting angry ❑ *I am to hull
here a little longer. Some mollification
for your giant* (*Twelfth Night 1.5*)

mouth, cold in the PHRASE a
well-known saying of the time which
meant to be dead ❑ *What, must our
mouths be cold?* (*The Tempest 1.1*)

murmur NOUN murmur was another
word for rumour or hearsay ❑ *and
then 'twas fresh in murmur* (*Twelfth
Night 1.2*)

murrain NOUN murrain was
another word for plague, pestilence
❑ *A murrain on your monster, and
the devil take your fingers!* (*The
Tempest 3.2*)

neaf NOUN neaf meant fist ❑ *Give
me your neaf, Monsieur Mustardseed*
(*A Midsummer Night's Dream 4.1*)

nice 1 ADJ nice had a number of
meanings here it means fussy or
particular ❑ *An therefore, goaded
with most sharp occasions,/ Which
lay nice manners by, I put you to/ The
use of your own virtues* (*All's Well
That Ends Well 5.1*) 2 ADJ nice here
means critical or delicate ❑ *We're
good… To set so rich a man/ On the
nice hazard of one doubtful hour?*
(*Henry IV part 1*) 3 ADJ nice in this
context means carefully accurate,
fastidious ❑ *O relation/ Too nice and
yet too true!* (*Macbeth 4.3*) 4 ADJ
trivial, unimportant ❑ *Romeo .. Bid
him bethink/ How nice the quarrel was*
(*Romeo and Juliet 3.1*)

nonpareil NOUN if you are
nonpareil you are without equal,
peerless ❑ *though you were crown'd/
The nonpareil of beauty!* (*Twelfth
Night 1.5*)

office NOUN office here means
business or work ❑ *Speak your office*
(*Twelfth Night 1.5*)

outsport VERB outsport meant
to overdo ❑ *Let's teach ourselves
that honorable stop,/ Not to outsport
discretion.* (*Othello 2.2*)

owe VERB owe meant own, possess
❑ *Lend less than thou owest* (*King
Lear 1.4*)

paragon 1 VERB to paragon was to
surpass or excede ❑ *he hath achieved
a maid/ That paragons description
and wild fame* (*Othello 2.1*) 2 VERB
to paragon could also mean to
compare with ❑ *I will give thee*

bloody teeth If thou with Caesar paragon again/ My man of men (Anthony and Cleopatra 1.5)

pate NOUN pate is another word for head ❑ *Back, slave, or I will break thy pate across* (The Comedy of Errors 2.1)

paunch VERB to paunch someone is to stab (usually in the stomach). Paunch is still a common word for a stomach ❑ *Batter his skull, or paunch him with a stake* (The Tempest 3.2)

peevish ADJ if you are peevish you are irritable or easily angered ❑ *Run after that same peevish messenger* (Twelfth Night 1.5)

peradventure ADV perhaps or maybe ❑ *Peradventure this is not Fortune's work* (As You Like It 1.2)

perforce 1 ADV by force or violently ❑ *my rights and royalties,/ Plucked from my arms perforce* (Richard II 2.3) 2 ADV necessarily ❑ *The hearts of men, they must perforce have melted* (Richard II 5.2)

personage NOUN personage meant your appearance ❑ *Of what personage and years is he?* (Twelfth Night 1.5)

pestilence NOUN pestilence was a common word for plague or disease ❑ *Methought she purg'd the air of pestilence!* (Twelfth Night 1.1)

physic NOUN physic was medicine or a treatment ❑ *tis a physic/ That's bitter to sweet end* (Measure for Measure 4.6)

place NOUN place means a person's position or rank ❑ *Sons, kinsmen, thanes,/ And you whose places are the nearest* (Macbeth 1.4)

post NOUN here a post means a messenger ❑ *there are twenty weak and wearied posts/ Come from the north* (Henry IV part II 2.4)

pox NOUN pox was a word for any disease during which the victim had blisters on the skin. It was also a curse, a swear word ❑ *The pox of such antic, lisping, affecting phantasims* (Romeo and Juliet 2.4)

prate VERB to prate means to chatter ❑ *if thou prate of mountains* (Hamlet 5.1)

prattle VERB to prattle is to chatter or talk without purpose ❑ *I prattle out of fashion, and I dote In mine own comforts* (Othello 2.1)

precept NOUN a precept was an order or command ❑ *and my father's precepts I therein do forget.* (The Tempest 3.1)

present ADJ present here means immediate ❑ *We'll put the matter to the present push* (Hamlet 5.1)

prithee EXCLAM prithee is the equivalent of please or may I ask – a polite request ❑ *I prithee, and I'll pay thee bounteously* (Twelfth Night 1.2)

prodigal NOUN a prodigal is someone who wastes or squanders money ❑ *he's a very fool, and a prodigal* (Twelfth Night 1.3)

purpose NOUN purpose is used here to mean intention ❑ *understand my purposes aright* (King Lear 1.4)

quaff VERB quaff was a common word which meant to drink heavily or take a big drink ❑ *That quaffing and drinking will undo you* (Twelfth Night 1.3)

quaint 1 ADJ clever, ingenious ❏ *with a quaint device* (*The Tempest 3.3*) 2 ADJ cunning ❏ *I'll… tell quaint lies* (*Merchant of Venice 3.4*) 3 ADJ pretty, attractive ❏ *The clamorous owl, that nightly hoots and wonders/At our quaint spirit* (*A Midsummer Night's Dream 2.2*)

quoth VERB an old word which means say ❏ *'Tis dinner time.' quoth I* (*The Comedy of Errors 2.1*)

rack NOUN a rack described clouds or a cloud formation ❏ *And, like this insubstantial pageant faded,/ Leave not a rack behind* (*The Tempest 4.1*)

rail VERB to rant or swear at. It is still used occasionally today ❏ *Why do I rail on thee* (*Richard II 5.5*)

rate NOUN rate meant estimate, opinion ❏ *My son is lost, and, in my rate, she too* (*The Tempest 2.1*)

recreant NOUN recreant is an old word which means coward ❏ *Come, recreant, come, thou child* (*A Midsummer Night's Dream 3.2*)

remembrance NOUN remembrance is used here to mean memory or recollection ❏ *our remembrances of days foregone* (*All's Well That Ends Well 1.3*)

resolute ADJ firm or not going to change your mind ❏ *You are resolute, then?* (*Twelfth Night 1.5*)

revels NOUN revels means celebrations or a party ❏ *Our revels now are ended* (*The Tempest 4.1*)

rough-cast NOUN a mixture of lime and gravel (sometimes shells too) for use on an outer wall ❏ *and let him have some plaster, or some loam, or some rough-cast about him, to signify wall* (*A Midsummer Night's Dream 3.1*)

sack NOUN sack was another word for wine ❏ *My man-monster hath drowned his tongue in sack.* (*The Tempest 3.2*)

sad ADJ in this context sad means serious, grave ❏ *comes me the Prince and Claudio… in sad conference* (*Much Ado About Nothing 1.3*)

sampler NOUN a piece of embroidery, which often showed the family tree ❏ *Both on one sampler, sitting on one cushion* (*A Midsummer Night's Dream 3.2*)

saucy ADJ saucy means rude ❏ *I heard you were saucy at my gates* (*Twelfth Night 1.5*)

schooling NOUN schooling means advice ❏ *I have some private schooling for you both.* (*A Midsummer Night's Dream 1.1*)

seething ADJ seething in this case means boiling – we now use seething when we are very angry ❏ *Lovers and madmen have such seething brains* (*A Midsummer Night's Dream 5.1*)

semblative ADJ semblative means resembling or looking like ❏ *And all is semblative a woman's part.* (*Twelfth Night 1.4*)

several ADJ several here means separate or different ❏ *twenty several messengers* (*Anthony and Cleopatra 1.5*)

shrew NOUN An annoying person or someone who makes you cross ❏ *Bless you, fair shrew.* (*Twelfth Night 1.3*)

shroud VERB to shroud is to hide or shelter ❑ *I will here, shroud till the dregs of the storm be past* (*The Tempest* 2.2)

sickleman NOUN a sickleman was someone who used a sickle to harvest crops ❑ *You sunburnt sicklemen, of August weary* (*The Tempest* 4.1)

soft ADV soft here means wait a moment or stop ❑ *But, soft, what nymphs are these* (*A Midsummer Night's Dream* 4.1)

something ADV something here means somewhat or rather ❑ *Be something scanter of your maiden presence* (*Hamlet* 1.3)

sooth NOUN truly ❑ *Yes, sooth; and so do you* (*A Midsummer Night's Dream* 3.2)

spleen NOUN spleen means fury or anger ❑ *That, in a spleen, unfolds both heaven and earth* (*A Midsummer Night's Dream* 1.1)

sport NOUN sport means recreation or entertainment ❑ *I see our wars/ Will turn unto a peaceful comic sport* (*Henry VI part I* 2.2)

strain NOUN a strain is a tune or a musical phrase ❑ *and so die/That strain again! it had a dying fall* (*Twelfth Night* 1.1)

suffer VERB in this context suffer means perish or die ❑ *but an islander that hath lately suffered by a thunderbolt.* (*The Tempest* 2.2)

suit NOUN a suit is a petition, request or proposal (marriage) ❑ *Because she will admit no kind of suit* (*Twelfth Night* 1.2)

sup VERB to sup is to have supper ❑ *Go know of Cassio where he supped tonight* (*Othello* 5.1)

surfeit NOUN a surfeit is an amount which is too large ❑ *If music be the food of love, play on;/Give me excess of it, that, surfeiting,/The appetite may sicken* (*Twelfth Night* 1.1)

swain NOUN a swain is a suitor or person who wants to marry ❑ *take this transformed scalp/From off the head of this Athenian swain* (*A Midsummer Night's Dream* 4.1)

thereto ADV thereto meant also ❑ *If she be black, and thereto have a wit* (*Othello* 2.1)

throstle NOUN a throstle was a name for a song-bird ❑ *The throstle with his note so true* (*A Midsummer Night's Dream* 3.1)

tidings NOUN tidings meant news ❑ *that upon certain tidings now arrived, importing the mere perdition of the Turkish fleet* (*Othello* 2.2)

transgress VERB if you transgress you break a moral law or rule of behaviour ❑ *Virtue that transgresses is but patched with sin* (*Twelfth Night* 1.5)

troth, by my PHRASE this phrase means I swear or in truth or on my word ❑ *By my troth, Sir Toby, you must come in earlier o' nights* (*Twelfth Night* 1.3)

trumpery NOUN trumpery means things that look expensive but are worth nothing (often clothing) ❑ *The trumpery in my house, go bring it hither/For stale catch these thieves* (*The Tempest* 4.1)

twink NOUN In the wink of an eye or no time at all ❑ *Ay, with a twink* (*The Tempest* 4.1)

undone ADJ if something or someone is undone they are ruined, destroyed, brought down ❑ *You have undone a man of fourscore three* (The Winter's Tale 4.4)

varlets NOUN varlets were villains or ruffians ❑ *Say again: where didst thou leave these varlets?* (The Tempest 4.1)

vaward NOUN the vaward is an old word for the vanguard, front part or earliest ❑ *And since we have the vaward of the day* (A Midsummer Night's Dream 4.1)

visage NOUN face ❑ *when Phoebe doth behold/Her silver visage in the watery glass* (A Midsummer Night's Dream 1.1)

voice NOUN voice means vote ❑ *He has our voices* (Coriolanus 2.3)

waggish ADJ waggish means playful ❑ *As waggish boys in game themselves forswear* (A Midsummer Night's Dream 1.1)

wane VERB to wane is to vanish, go down or get slighter. It is most often used to describe a phase of the moon ❑ *but, O, methinks, how slow/This old moon wanes* (A Midsummer Night's Dream 1.1)

want VERB to want means to lack or to be without ❑ *a beast that wants discourse of reason/Would have mourned longer* (Hamlet 1.2)

warrant VERB to assure, promise, guarantee ❑ *I warrant your grace* (As You Like It 1.2)

welkin NOUN welkin is an old word for the sky or the heavens ❑ *The starry welkin cover thou anon/With drooping fog as black as Acheron* (A Midsummer Night's Dream 3.2)

wench NOUN wench is an old word for a girl ❑ *Well demanded, wench* (The Tempest 1.2)

whence ADV from where ❑ *Whence came you, sir?* (Twelfth Night 1.5)

wherefore ADV why ❑ *Wherefore, sweetheart? what's your metaphor?* (Twelfth Night 1.3)

wide-chopped ADJ if you were wide-chopped you were big-mouthed ❑ *This wide-chopped rascal* (The Tempest 1.1)

wight NOUN wight is an old word for person or human being ❑ *She was a wight, if ever such wight were* (Othello 2.1)

wit NOUN wit means intelligence or wisdom ❑ *thou didst conclude hairy men plain dealers, without wit* (The Comedy of Errors 2.2)

wits NOUN wits mean mental sharpness ❑ *we that have good wits have much to answer for* (As You Like It 4.1)

wont ADJ to wont is to be in the habit of doing something regularly ❑ *When were you wont to use my sister thus?* (The Comedy of Errors 2.2)

wooer NOUN a wooer is a suitor, someone who is hoping to marry ❑ *and of a foolish knight that you brought in one night here to be her wooer* (Twelfth Night 1.3)

wot VERB wot is an old word which means know or learn ❑ *for well I wot/Thou runnest before me* (A Midsummer Night's Dream 3.2)